McDougal Littell

Strategies *for* Test Preparation

MIDDLE SCHOOL

McDougal Littell
A HOUGHTON MIFFLIN COMPANY
Evanston, Illinois • Boston • Dallas

Acknowledgments

Page 13: Excerpt from *The Analects of Confucius,* translated and annotated by Simon Lays.
Copyright © 1997 Pierre Rychmans. All rights reserved. Reprinted by permission of W. W. Norton & Company, Inc.

Page 21: Daniel Fitzpatrick cartoon: "Next!" Swastica rolling over Poland. Reprinted with permission of the Saint Louis Post-Dispatch, 2001.

Page 22: King Andrew the First cartoon. Library of Congress

Page 23: Berlin Wall cartoon, Jeff Koterba, 1989. Copyright © Jeff Koterba/Omaha World Herald

Page 49: Ghandi marching against salt tax, 1930. Copyright © Mansell Collection/Time, Inc.

Page 57: Mongol Warrior. Copyright © Victoria & Albert Museum, London/Art Resource, NY.

Page 59: Dominic Fruscello, West Genesee High School, Camillus New York

Page 65: View of San Francisco [Formerly Yerba Buena] (1847), attributed to Victor Prevost. Oil on canvas, 25" × 30". California Historical Society, gift of the Ohio Historical Society

Page 65: San Francisco, photo of the city in 1850. The Bancroft Library, University of California, Berkeley.

Copyright © by McDougal Littell Inc. All rights reserved.

Permission is hereby granted to teachers to reprint or photocopy in classroom quantities the pages or sheets in this work that carry a McDougal Littell copyright notice. These pages are designed to be reproduced by teachers for use in their classes with accompanying McDougal Littell material, provided each copy made shows the copyright notice. Such copies may not be sold, and further distribution is expressly prohibited. Except as authorized above, prior written permission must be obtained from McDougal Littell Inc. to reproduce or transmit this work or portions thereof in any other form or by any other electronic or mechanical means, including any information storage or retrieval system, unless expressly permitted by federal copyright law. Address inquiries to Manager, Rights and Permissions, McDougal Littell Inc., P.O. Box 1667, Evanston, IL 60204.

ISBN 0-618-15938-X

Printed in the United States of America.
 3 4 5 6 7 8 9 - MDO - 06 05 04

Table of Contents

PART 1

Introduction 1
General Strategies for Taking Tests 2–8

PART 2

Test-Taking Strategies and Practice 9–68
    Multiple Choice 9–12
    Primary Sources 13–16
    Secondary Sources 17–20
    Political Cartoons 21–24
    Charts 25–28
    Line and Bar Graphs 29–32
    Bar Graphs 33–36
    Physical Maps 37–40
    Thematic Maps 41–44
    Time Lines 45–48
    Constructed Response 49–52
    Extended Response 53–56
    Document-Based Questions 57–68

PART 3

Sample Test Questions 69–87
    Sample Test Questions 72–85
    Answer Key 86–87

INTRODUCTION

Strategies for Test Preparation

You can prepare for tests as you would for any other assignment you are given during the school year. The materials in this booklet will boost your achievement level in history and social science.

Content Overview

Each part of this booklet gives a different type of support that can become part of your daily study habits.

Part 1: General Strategies for Taking Tests

Tips for Successful Testing This section gives strategies you can use during the school year to help you prepare for tests. It also provides tips you can use during the testing.

Vocabulary for Testing Situations In this section you'll find brief definitions of words often used on tests and terms taught in social science texts.

Part 2: Test-Taking Strategies and Practice

This part of the book provides tutorials and practice in the types of items that appear on many types of social studies tests. Each tutorial offers instruction and practice in the content areas of world geography, world history, or U.S. history. Practice items usually include an *exhibit* of some sort, followed by multiple-choice, constructed-response, or extended-response questions—and you'll even have a chance to practice writing for a document-based question (DBQ). Exhibits include:

- Primary sources
- Secondary sources
- Political cartoons
- Charts
- Time lines
- Physical maps
- Thematic maps4
- Pie graphs
- Line graphs and bar graphs

Part 2: Test-Taking Strategies and Practice

This part of the book provides practice that will help you perform well on various types of questions commonly found on social studies tests. There are 49 practice questions that cover material that will increase your knowledge of history. After you have taken the practice test, check your answers to see how well you did. Take notice of the types of questions you missed and return to the strategies practice pages to improve your skill in answering questions.

Part 1: General Strategies for Taking Tests

Tips for Successful Testing

There are many ways you can prepare for tests. These practices can reinforce your daily learning in class, both in social studies and in other content areas. Knowledge of test-taking techniques doesn't replace knowledge of content, but it can help you learn how to use the test to demonstrate what you really know. You shouldn't lose points simply because you don't know how to take a test. The following tips give you some general suggestions on how to approach a test; you'll find more detailed instruction and practice in Part 2: Test-Taking Strategies and Practice.

During the School Year

1. **Master the content of your social studies courses.** The best way to study for tests is to study, understand, and review the content of your social studies class, whether you're taking history, geography, government, or economics. Read your daily assignments carefully, and review the text and your classroom notes on a weekly basis. If you do these, you will do well on tests.

2. **Practice with testing vocabulary.** Review the lists given in the next few pages. Your teacher may build some of these words into informal and formal assessments. For words that can be used in a variety of ways, make sure you understand the particular meaning the words have in the context of testing. Try to use history/social science vocabulary during class and in homework assignments.

3. **Practice taking tests.** Use copies of past tests to practice taking a test with time limits. Learning how to effectively use your time is an important test-taking skill.

4. **Practice reading and interpreting visual representations of information.** Your textbook has many examples of charts, graphs, maps, political cartoons, and graphic organizers. Become familiar with how these visuals work, and the ways in which they present information.

5. **Interact with your own textbook.** Practice responding to assessment questions in your textbook, both orally and in writing. Try summarizing or paraphrasing longer passages.

6. **Build your stamina for long testing sessions.**
   a. Brainstorm appropriate ways to take short breaks during a timed session. You can try deep breathing, stretching, and so on.
   b. Think of strategies you've used before when you've had to concentrate for a long interval, and see how they might be applied to the testing situation.

7. **Learn to analyze the test questions.** Often, test questions seem awkward because they are written using language and/or formats that are unfamiliar or uncommon.
   a. Try paraphrasing the question in order to better understand it.
   b. Identify the type of information asked for in each question.

8. **Learn to skim materials.** Practice running your eyes quickly over texts, looking at headings, graphic features, and highlighted words. Learn to pick key words and phrases out of materials.

9. **Discuss test experiences immediately afterward.** After classroom tests and quizzes throughout the year, talk with your teacher and classmates about the experience. What strategies did you and your classmates use to come up with your answers? Were your choices effective?

PART 1

Strategies for Test Preparation

Several Weeks Before the Test

As the date for a test approaches, begin to prepare specifically for the types of items you might find in the test. Here are general tips for item types that you'll have a chance to practice answering later in this book.

1. **Multiple-Choice Questions** Remember, test writers may set traps. In a well-constructed item, each wrong answer represents a mistake that might be made by a test taker who is careless or doesn't know the material. Use the following strategies with multiple-choice items.

   a. Read and consider the question (this part is called the *stem*) carefully *before* reading the alternative answers.

   b. Pay close attention to key words in the question. For instance, look for the word *not*, as in "Which of the following was *not* a cause of the Civil War?"

   c. Consider all the alternatives before making a choice.

   d. Eliminate any answers that you know are wrong. Often you will be able to eliminate alternatives that are weaker than the others, leaving a choice between the strongest two.
      - Look for two choices that appear to boil down to the same idea. Both must be wrong.
      - Read the stem and each answer as a sentence. Does this sentence make grammatical and logical sense? Eliminate alternatives that do not "read in" logically.
      - When an answer is over qualified, it may be incorrect. Look for words like *always, never, none, all,* and *only* as a tip-off.

   e. When in doubt about an answer, try these ideas to find the correct answer:
      - If one choice is much longer and more detailed than the others, it is often the correct answer.
      - If a word in a choice also appears in the question, it should be strongly considered as the correct choice.
      - If two choices are direct opposites, one of them likely is the correct answer.
      - If one choice includes one or more of the other choices, it is often the correct answer.
      - If *some* or *often* is used in a choice, it should be strongly considered as the correct answer.
      - If *all of the above* is a choice, determine whether at least two of the other choices seem appropriate before selecting it.
      - If one response is more precise or technical, it is more likely to be correct than a general response.

2. **Constructed-Response Items** Constructed-response items can have many forms. You may have to read a paragraph, graph, chart, map, or graphic organizer to extract information, and to make an inference or draw a conclusion. You might have to create a map, graph, or graphic organizer yourself. Use these strategies for approaching a constructed-response item.

   a. Read the directions and analyze the steps required. Read through the entire question or questions before answering.

   b. Look for key words in the prompt and plan your answer accordingly. Does the question ask you to identify a cause-and-effect relationship or to compare and contrast? Are you looking for a sequence or making a generalization?

PART 1

Strategies for Test Preparation

    c. **Plan your answer.** If you are writing more than a few words, jot down notes and supporting details you may wish to use in your response.

    d. **Target your answer.** When writing your response, don't just include everything you can think of, hoping that some part of it will be correct.

    e. Support your statements with examples and details.

3. **Extended-Response Items** Extended-response questions, like constructed-response questions, usually focus on a document of some kind. However, they are more complex and require more time to complete than short-answer constructed-response questions. Use the following strategies with extended-response items.

    a. Carefully read the question and determine what it asks you to do.

    b. Analyze the document and make notes on material that may apply to the question.

    c. If the question requires an essay or other piece of writing, jot down ideas in outline form. Use the outline to write your answer.

During Test Administration

Keep the following points in mind while taking a test.

1. **Read the directions.** There may be slight differences among similar directions that could make a significant difference.

2. **Take a second look.** Recheck your answers to make sure you haven't made a mistake in your markings.

3. **Pay special attention when using a separate answer sheet.** It is easy to drop down one line and accidentally throw off the answers. Use any or all of the following techniques.

    a. Use a guide, such as a ruler, on the answer sheet to keep from marking answers on the wrong line.

    b. Check every five answers or so to make sure that the appropriate line is filled for each answer.

    c. Each time you turn a page, make sure the question and answer lines match.

    d. Fill in blanks carefully and neatly and beware of stray pencil marks.

    e. Fold the test booklet so that only one page is showing at a time.

4. **As a last resort, make an educated guess.** When there is no penalty for guessing on a multiple-choice item, it's better to guess at an answer than to leave it blank. Try to eliminate one or two choices first.

5. **Rely on facts or data in the question**—not on personal preferences—when answering questions. Pay close attention to information provided in graphs, charts, or quotations when coming up with your answer.

6. **Ration your time.** Answering all of the questions will increase your chances for a better score, so you should make sure to finish the test. Pay attention to the time, and work to maintain an appropriate pace. Calculate in advance how many questions you need to answer by the halfway mark, but remember that some question formats may take you longer than others.

PART 1 Strategies for Test Preparation

Vocabulary for Testing Situations

The following vocabulary words can help you prepare for tests. The first vocabulary list contains words often used in test materials. The accompanying definitions show how each word would most likely be used in a test situation, but may not be the only definitions.

The second list consists of vocabulary words taken from social studies textbooks. They are words that might prove helpful in testing situations.

Test Vocabulary

according to as stated in
action act, step, endeavor
affect influence, change
analyze break down into parts and explain relationships
apparent clear, obvious
appropriate suitable, correct
argument reason offered in proof for or against an idea
characterize represent, symbolize, show qualities of
classified arranged into groups according to specific categories
combined joined, united
compare/contrast explore similarities and differences
condition situation, circumstances
contribute add to, assist
correspond to conform, match, fit
current at the present time
data information, facts, figures
define give the exact meaning of
depend upon be determined by
describe give key information about
determine decide
development progress, growth
draw a conclusion make a judgment based on certain ideas/facts
emphasize stress, focus on, feature
evaluate judge the value of
event something that happens in a particular time/place
example illustration, representation
except all but, everything other than
excerpt selection, portion of a text
expanding growing, increasing
explain make clear and understandable
former previous, earlier
foundation base, support for conclusion
generalization general statement based on many examples
graph visual representation of facts/figures

Part 1 General Strategies for Taking Tests **5**

PART 1

Strategies for Test Preparation

identify find, pick out
impact affect, influence
indicate show, point out
inference a conclusion based on deduction, an informed guess
intend plan, design
interpret give your opinion, supported with reasons and details
involve be a part of
major significant, important
minor small, insignificant
occur happen
passage part of a written work, text
point location, position, main idea
primary main, most important
principle a basic law or truth
probably most likely
provide offer, supply
refer to use as a source of information
regulate control, manage
relate show the relationship or link between things
result findings, report
select choose
sequence order, arrangement
significant important, meaningful
similar nearly alike
topic subject
valid logical, suitable

History/Social Studies Vocabulary

Civics/Government

administration a particular president's term of office
Bill of Rights first ten amendments to the U.S. Constitution
bureaucracy a system of departments and agencies that carry out the work of the government
checks and balances measures designed to prevent one branch of the government from dominating another
elector a voter
impeachment the process of accusing a public official of wrongdoing
judicial review Supreme Court's power to declare an act of Congress unconstitutional
legislation law, bill, statute
naturalization a way to give full citizenship to a person born in another country
ruling official or legal decision
suffrage the right to vote
treaty agreement between nations

PART 1

Strategies for Test Preparation

Culture
civilization a form of culture characterized by cities, specialized workers, complex institutions, record keeping, and advanced technology
culture a people's unique way of life
ethnic racial, cultural
population citizens, people
society community, a social order
system organization, structure
urban relating to cities or towns

Economics
capitalism economic system based on private ownership and the investment of money for profit
communism economic and political system based on one-party government and state ownership of property and production
demand willingness and ability of consumers to spend money for goods and services
economy system for the management of resources
depression a severe economic slump
free enterprise economic system in which business can be conducted freely based on the choices of individuals
goods material things that can be bought and sold
inflation an increase in the price of goods and services and a decrease in the value of money
recession an economic slump, less severe than a depression
services work performed for others
share portion of a company's stock
supply amount of economic goods available for sale
tariff a tax on imported goods
taxes money paid to the government for its support

Geography
area region, section of land bound by common characteristics
boundary border, dividing line
canyon a narrow, deep valley with steep sides
cape a pointed piece of land extending into an ocean or lake
climate conditions, such as wind, rainfall, and temperature, that are common in a region
delta a marshy region formed by silt deposits at the mouth of a river
desert a dry area where few plants grow
desertification transformation of fertile land into desert
environment habitat, climate
flood plain flat land near the edges of rivers formed by mud and silt deposited by floods
glacier a large ice mass that moves slowly down a mountain or over land
harbor a sheltered area of water deep enough for docking ships
hemisphere half of the globe
island a body of land surrounded by water
latitude distance in degrees north or south of the earth's equator

PART 1 — Strategies for Test Preparation

location position
longitude distance in degrees east or west of the prime meridian at Greenwich, England
plateau a broad, flat area of land higher than the surrounding land
prairie a large, level area of grassland with few or no trees
projection a way of showing the curved surface of the earth on a flat map
region geographical area
scale ratio between a unit of length on a map and a unit of distance on the earth
steppe a wide, treeless plain
strait a narrow strip of water connecting two large bodies of water
swamp an area of land that is saturated by water
valley low land between hills or mountains
volcano an opening in the earth through which gasses and lava escape from the earth's interior

History

apartheid South African policy of complete legal and social separation of the races
aristocracy government in which the power is in the hands of a hereditary ruling class or nobility
Cold War state of diplomatic hostility between the United States and the Soviet Union in the decades following World War II
fascism political movement that promotes extreme forms of nationalism, denial of individual rights, and dictatorial one-party rule
immigration entering and settling in a country of which one is not a native
imperialism policy in which a strong nation seeks to dominate other countries socially, economically, or politically.
Industrial Revolution the shift from making goods by hand to making them by machine
industrialization development of industries for the machine production of goods
isolationism policy of avoiding political or military involvement with other countries
nationalism belief that people should be loyal mainly to their nation rather than to a king or an emperor
Nazism fascist policies of National Socialist German Workers' party, based on totalitarianism and belief in racial superiority
New Deal Franklin Roosevelt's economic reform program designed to solve the problems of the Great Depression
period a span of time, a number of years tied together by common elements
Reconstruction the period of rebuilding following the Civil War
segregation separation of people based on race
time line line that lists, in order, events and the dates on which they occurred
totalitarianism policy of government control over all aspects of public and private life

STRATEGIES

Strategies for Test Preparation

Part 2: Test-Taking Strategies and Practice

Multiple Choice

A multiple-choice question consists of a stem and a set of choices. The stem is usually in the form of a question or an incomplete sentence. One of the choices correctly answers the question or completes the sentence.

❶ Read the stem carefully and try to answer the question or complete the sentence without looking at the choices.

❷ Pay close attention to key words in the stem. They may direct you toward the correct answer.

❸ Read each choice with the stem. Don't jump to conclusions about the correct answer until you've read all of the choices.

❹ Think carefully about questions that include *All of the above* among the choices.

❺ After reading all of the choices, eliminate any that you know are incorrect.

❻ Use modifiers to help narrow your choice.

❼ Look for the best answer among the remaining choices.

Improve your test-taking skills by practicing the strategies discussed in this section. Read the tips on the strategies page. Then apply them to the practice items on the next two pages. Use the Thinking Through the Answers page that follows the practice pages to help you evaluate your answers to the practice items.

United States History Sample

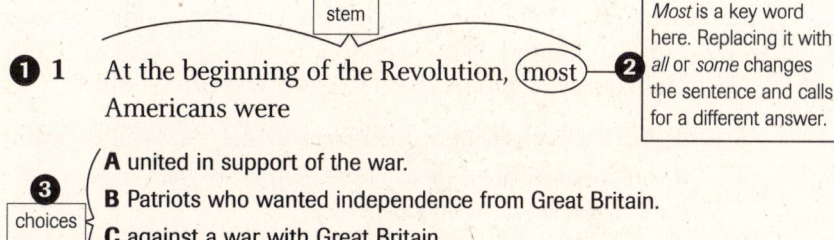

❶ 1. At the beginning of the Revolution, most Americans were

❸ choices:
- A united in support of the war.
- B Patriots who wanted independence from Great Britain.
- C against a war with Great Britain.
- D Loyalists who supported the British point of view.

❷ *Most* is a key word here. Replacing it with *all* or *some* changes the sentence and calls for a different answer.

2. Which of the following weapons were first used effectively during World War I?

- A Airplanes
- B Machine guns
- C Tanks
- D All of the above

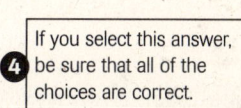 ❹ If you select this answer, be sure that all of the choices are correct.

3. At the outset of the Civil War, both the Union and the Confederacy wanted the support of the border states—

- A Delaware, Maryland, Kentucky, and Oklahoma.
- B Delaware, Maryland, Kentucky, and Missouri.
- C Delaware, Maryland, West Virginia, Kentucky, and Missouri.
- D all the states bordering the Missouri Compromise line.

❺ You can eliminate **A** if you remember that Oklahoma was not a state at the time of the Civil War.

❻ Absolute words, such as *all, never, always, every,* and *only,* often signal an incorrect choice.

❼ In **C**, West Virginia did lie on the border between the Union and the Confederacy. However, it broke away from Virginia early in the war and became a state in 1863. Therefore, **B** is the correct answer.

answers: 1 (C), 2 (D), 3 (B)

Part 2 Test-Taking Strategies and Practice 9

PRACTICE

Strategies for Test Preparation

United States History Sample

Directions: Read each question carefully and choose the *best* answer from the four choices.

1. The conflict that gave Great Britain control of much of North America was the

   A War of 1812.
   B Spanish-American War.
   C French and Indian War.
   D Revolutionary War.

2. The Louisiana Purchase of 1803 gave the United States

   A all of the land west of the Mississippi River.
   B only the land that makes up modern-day Louisiana.
   C the region known as the Ohio Valley.
   D much of the land between the Mississippi River and Rocky Mountains.

3. The invention that boosted the Southern economy and prompted the spread of slavery was the

   A cotton gin.
   B telegraph.
   C steel plow.
   D reaper.

4. Which of the following did NOT play a role in bringing an end to Reconstruction?

   A the Compromise of 1877
   B the Fifteenth Amendment
   C the Panic of 1873
   D Supreme Court reversals of Reconstruction acts

PRACTICE

Strategies for Test Preparation

World Cultures and Geography Sample

Directions: Read each question carefully and choose the *best* answer from the four choices.

1. The early African kingdom of Aksum became a powerful trading center due in part to its location along the

   A Red Sea.
   B Black Sea.
   C Baltic Sea.
   D Mediterranean Sea.

2. Islam is a religion based on the teachings of

   A Confucius.
   B Jesus Christ.
   C Muhammad.
   D Siddhartha Guatama.

3. All of the following were characteristics of Aztec society EXCEPT

   A the use of slaves.
   B a democratic form of government.
   C a major urban center.
   D religious ceremonies involving human sacrifice.

4. As a result of the Columbian Exchange

   A Europeans were introduced to corn and tomatoes.
   B the horse was introduced to the Americas.
   C Native Americans were exposed to smallpox and other diseases.
   D All of the above

ANSWERS

Strategies for Test Preparation

Thinking Through the Answers

QUESTIONS FROM PAGE 10:

1. **C** is correct. Remember that Great Britain and France were in conflict for control of North America.

   A and **B** are incorrect. These wars took place after the United States became an independent nation and Great Britain no longer controlled North America.
   D is incorrect. This war gave the American colonists their independence from Great Britain.

2. **D** is the correct answer. The Louisiana Purchase extended west from the Mississippi River.

   A and **B** are incorrect. Extreme words such as *all* and *only* usually signal an incorrect answer.
   C is incorrect. The United States already had settled the Ohio Valley region by 1800.

3. **A** is correct. The cotton gin made cleaning cotton easier and led to a jump in production and the demand for slaves to work the cotton fields.

   B is incorrect. The telegraph improved communication, not the Southern economy or slavery.
   C and **D** are incorrect. These inventions aided farmers on the dry and hard plains of the West.

4. The question asks for the event or act that *did not* play a role in ending Reconstruction.

   B is correct. The Fifteenth Amendment guaranteed African Americans the right to vote. It was a key measure of Reconstruction, not an act that led to its end.
   A is incorrect. The Compromise of 1877 played the most direct role in ending Reconstruction.
   C and **D** are incorrect. Both of these are considered long-term causes of the end of Reconstruction.

QUESTIONS FROM PAGE 11:

1. Aksum was a kingdom in northeastern Africa, a region that borders the Red Sea.

   A is correct.
   B and **C** are incorrect. The Black Sea and Baltic Sea are located near Europe, not Africa.
   D is incorrect. The Mediterranean Sea, along Africa's northern border, did not touch Aksum.

2. **C** is correct. Islam is based on the teachings of the prophet Muhammad.

   A, B, and **D** are not correct. Confucius was the originator of Confucianism, the teachings of Jesus Christ led to the formation of Christianity, and Siddhartha Guatama, who became known as the Buddha, was the founder of Buddhism.

3. The question asks for an aspect that was *not* a characteristic of Aztec society.

   B is correct. Democracy did not exist in the Aztec empire; it was ruled by an emperor whose power was absolute.
   A, C, and **D** are incorrect because they are characteristics of Aztec society.

4. **D** is correct. Because all three answers are effects of the Columbian Exchange, All of the above is the correct answer.

STRATEGIES

Strategies for Test Preparation

Primary Sources

Sometimes you will need to look at a document to answer a question. Some documents are primary sources. Primary sources are written or made by people who either saw an event or were actually part of the event. A primary source can be a photograph, letter, diary, speech, or autobiography.

❶ Look at the source line to learn about the document and its author. If the author is well known and has been quoted a lot, the information is probably true.

❷ Skim the article to get an idea of what it is about.

❸ Note any special punctuation. For example, ellipses (. . .) indicate that words and sentences have been left out.

❹ Ask yourself questions about the document as you read.

❺ Review the questions. This will give your reading a purpose and also help you find the answers more easily. Then reread the document.

World Cultures and Geography Sample

Good Government

Chap 2.20 Lord Ji Kang asked, "What should I do in order to make the people respectful, loyal, and zealous [hard-working]?" The Master said: "Approach them with dignity and they will be respectful. Be yourself a good son and kind father, and they will be loyal. Raise the good and train the incompetent, and they will be zealous."

Chap. 13.2 Ran Yong (. . .) asked about government. The Master said: "Guide the officials. Forgive small mistakes. Promote [people] of talent." "How does one recognize that a [person] has talent and deserves to be promoted?" The Master said: "Promote those you know. Those whom you do not know will hardly remain ignored."

—*The Analects of Confucius*

> The *Analects* is a book of thoughts and ideas by Confucius. He was a scholar and teacher in ancient China. **❶**

1 Confucius is giving advice on

   A how to be a gentleman.
   B how to be a good ruler.
   C how to become wealthy.
   D how to raise a good family.

2 Which sentence BEST expresses the idea of these paragraphs?

   A The wise ruler governs people through fear.
   B People should obey their rulers no matter what.
   C A good ruler gives a lot of orders to people.
   D If rulers do things well, people will follow them.

answers: 1 (B), 2 (D)

Excerpt from *The Analects of Confucius,* translated and annotated by Simon Leys. Copyright © 1997 by Pierre Ryckmans, All rights reserved. Reprinted by permission of W.W. Norton & Company, Inc.

Part 2 Test-Taking Strategies and Practice **13**

Name _____ Date _____

PRACTICE

Strategies for Test Preparation

World Cultures and Geography Sample

Directions: Below is an excerpt from a traveler to the Gobi Desert in Mongolia, a country just north of China. Use this passage and your knowledge of world cultures and geography to answer the questions.

> I was there in the summer because the living is easy, relatively. The temperature may get up to 100 in the shade, 145 in the midday sun, but in this high, dry land, the heat does not sap the will. For six months of the year, life is much harder. The winters drive the temperature down to [40 degrees below zero] . . . Then in the spring, when mountain and desert, barrens and grassland, north and south, all warm at different rates, air rises and flows with punishing force. Brutal cold gives way to sandblasting gales that can flay exposed skin and strip the paint from a car.
>
> —John Man, *Gobi*

1. According to the author, the best time to travel in the Gobi Desert is

   A winter.
   B spring.
   C summer.
   D fall.

2. Based on the author's account, the winds of the Gobi Desert can best be described as

   A weak.
   B strong.
   C smelly.
   D northerly.

3. What is the cause of the warming of the land at different rates?

   A altitude
   B location
   C ground cover
   D All of the above

Name _____   Date _____

PRACTICE

Strategies for Test Preparation

United States History Sample

Directions: Below is part of a 1776 letter from Abigail Adams to her husband John Adams on the eve of the colonists' declaration of independence from Great Britain. Use this passage and your knowledge of U.S. history to answer the questions.

> I long to hear the you have declared an independency—and by the way in the new Code of Laws which I suppose it will be necessary for you to make I desire you would Remember the Ladies, and be more generous and favorable to them than your ancestors. Do not put such unlimited power into the hands of the Husbands. Remember all Men would be tyrants if they could. If particular care and attention is not paid to the ladies we are determined to foment a Rebellion, and will not hold ourselves bound by any Laws in which we have no voice, or Representation.
>
> —Abigail Adams, quoted in *100 Key Documents in American Democracy*

1. Abigail Adams wants any new government in America to include greater rights and freedoms for

   A men.
   B women.
   C Native Americans.
   D African Americans.

2. In the nation's new government women were denied

   A the right to vote.
   B freedom of speech.
   C freedom of religion.
   D the right to work.

3. Abigail Adams mentions the creation of a new Code of Laws. What will that document be called?

   A Constitution
   B Declaration of Independence
   C Fundamental Orders
   D Mayflower Compact

Part 2 Test-Taking Strategies and Practice **15**

ANSWERS

Strategies for Test Preparation

Thinking Through the Answers

Questions from Page 14:

1. **C** is correct. The author describes the summer as the easiest time to be in the Gobi Desert compared to the other seasons.

   A and **B** are incorrect. The author says both of these seasons are difficult times to be there, as temperatures drop to minus 40 degrees in the winter and gale-force winds dominate the spring.

   D is incorrect. The author makes no mention of fall, and thus this distracter cannot be right.

2. **B** is correct. The author describes them as "sandblasting gales" and insists they could "strip the paint from a car."

   A is incorrect. The author views the winds as just the opposite of weak.

   C and **D** are incorrect. Nowhere in the passage is the smell or direction of the wind discussed, so neither answer is right.

3. **D** is correct. All of the factors listed affect the warming of the land at different rates.

   A, B, C are incorrect. Each of these factors causes warming at a different rate.

Questions from Page 15:

1. **B** is correct. The thrust of Abigail Adams's plea to her husband is to "Remember the Ladies" and to provide women with a greater voice in government.

   A is incorrect. According to Adams, men have too much power in society, and many of them behave like tyrants.

   C and **D** are incorrect. Nowhere in the excerpt does Adams mention Native Americans or African Americans, and thus neither answer is correct.

2. **A** is correct. As you recall, women were excluded from participating in the nation's new government.

   B and **C** are incorrect. Both of these rights are guaranteed for all citizens by the U.S. Constitution.

   D is incorrect. Neither Adams nor the Constitution mention the right to work.

3. **A** is correct. The code of laws written after Independence was the Constitution.

   B is incorrect. The Declaration of Independence was not a code of laws but an explanation of the colonists reasons for breaking away from England.

   C is incorrect. The Fundamental Orders applied to Connecticut only.

   D is incorrect. The Mayflower Compact applied to the Pilgrims in 1620.

STRATEGIES

Strategies for Test Preparation

Secondary Sources

A secondary source is an account of events by a person who did not actually experience them. The author often uses information from several primary sources to write about a person or event. Biographies, many newspaper articles, and history books are examples of secondary sources.

❶ Read the title to get an idea of what the passage is about. (The title here indicates that the passage is about a person named Malinche about whom people have different opinions.)

❷ Skim the paragraphs to find the main idea of the passage.

❸ Look for words that help you understand the order in which events happen.

❹ Ask yourself questions as you read. (You might ask yourself: Why did people's opinions about Malinche change over time?)

❺ Review the questions to see what information you will need to find. Then reread the passage.

World Cultures and Geography Sample

❶ Malinche—Heroine or Traitor?

No one knows much about Malinche's early life. People do know that in 1519 she met Hernán Cortés. The Spanish conquistador had landed in Mexico earlier that year. Malinche was only 15 years old. ❷ Even though she was very young, Malinche helped Cortés conquer the Aztecs. She spoke the languages of the Aztec and the Maya. Over time, she learned Spanish. She translated for Cortés and advised him on Native American politics.

The Spanish conquistadors admired Malinche, calling her Doña Marina. ❸ For many centuries, the Spanish people regarded her as a heroine. In the 1800s, however, Mexico won its independence from Spain. People rejected their Spanish rulers. Writers and artists started calling Malinche a traitor to her people. Today, however, she is seen as a heroine again. ❹

1 Which of the following statements about Malinche is an (opinion)?

Remember that an opinion is a statement that cannot be proved. A fact is a statement that can be proved.

A She was very young when she met Cortés.
B She became a translator for Cortés.
C She was a traitor to her own people.
D She understood Native American politics.

2 Based on this source, which person or group would view Malinche as a heroine?

A a fighter for Mexican independence from Spain
B the soldiers and officers in Cortés's army
C the Aztec ruler and his court in Mexico
D an historian writing about Mexico in the 1800s

answers: 1 (C), 2 (B)

Part 2 Test-Taking Strategies and Practice **17**

Name _____   Date _____

PRACTICE   Strategies for Test Preparation

World Cultures and Geography Sample

Directions: The Ch'in was the first dynasty to rule a unified China and its reign lasted from 221 b.c. to 206 B.C. Use this passage about the Ch'in and your knowledge of world cultures and geography to answer the questions.

Geography Helps the Ch'in

Among the important reasons for Ch'in's rise to power was its strategically advantageous [favorable] geographic location. Its home territory in modern Shensi province and the territory it absorbed in modern Szechwan province in 316 BC are . . . . well insulated [protected] from the east by mountains and gorges. . . [This] topography makes intrusion from the east difficult . . . The Ch'in heartland was never itself a major battleground.

Geography also gave Ch'in economic advantages, which it exploited expertly. The Shensi valley was renowned [well known] in early times as having the most productive soil in all China, and Ch'in was one of the first states to develop widespread irrigation systems. The annexation [addition] of Szechwan gave Ch'in another rich agricultural basin and excellent resources in minerals and lumber.

—Charles Hucker, *China's Imperial Past*

1   According to the passage, the Ch'in avoided military attacks due in large part to their location along a

   A river.
   B field.
   C mountain range.
   D desert.

2   The Ch'in's rich soil most likely enabled them to obtain much of their food by

   A farming.
   B hunting.
   C trading.
   D fishing.

3   What resources contributed to the Ch'in economy?

   A productive soil
   B lumber
   C water
   D All of the above

Name _____   Date _____

PRACTICE

Strategies for Test Preparation

United States History Sample

Directions: Use this passage about progressivism and your knowledge of U.S. history to answer the questions.

The Progressive Movement

The rapid growth of cities and industries in the United States at the turn of the twentieth century brought many problems. Among them were poverty, the spread of slums, and poor conditions in factories. In addition, corrupt political machines had won control of many city and state governments. Big business had gained power over the economy and government.

To attack these problems, individuals organized a number of reform movements. These reformers believed in the basic goodness of people. They also believed in democracy. The reformers were mostly native born and middle-class. They could be found in either political party. Their reform movements came to be grouped under the label progressivism. The progressive reformers shared at least one of three basic goals: first, to reform government and expand democracy; second, to promote social welfare; third, to create economic reform.

1   Progressive reformers could be found among

   A Democrats.
   B Republicans.
   C the middle class.
   D All of the above.

2   The cause of the problems progressive reformers faced was

   A slums.
   B industrialization.
   C poverty.
   D poor factory conditions.

3   Based on their goals, progressive reformers sought to do all of the following EXCEPT:

   A root out government corruption.
   B promote world peace.
   C improve conditions for the poor.
   D weaken the power of giant corporations.

Part 2 Test-Taking Strategies and Practice **19**

Name _____ Date _____

ANSWERS
Strategies for Test Preparation

Thinking Through the Answers

Questions from Page 18:

1. **C** is correct. As the passage states, the Ch'in were protected from the east by mountains, which make a military attack extremely difficult.

   A and **B** are incorrect. According to the passage, the Ch'in were not located along either a river or a field—and neither would be a much of a barrier against a military attack.

   D is incorrect. While a desert would make a formidable barrier against attack, there is no mention of a desert in the passage.

2. **A** is correct. The presence of rich soil meant that the land was ideal for growing crops, and thus the Ch'in most likely engaged in much farming.

   B and **C** are incorrect. With land suitable for farming, the Ch'in would most likely not have to hunt or trade for what they ate.

   D is incorrect. Because there is no mention of any bodies of water in the passage, you could assume that fishing is not the right answer.

3. **D** is correct because all of the resources listed were found in the Ch'in territory.

   A, B, C are incorrect. Each of these resources were found in the Ch'in territory.

Questions from Page 19:

1. **D** is correct. Because all three answers are traits of the progressive reformers, *All of the above* is the correct answer.

   A and **B** are incorrect. According to the passage, reformers came from either political party, which meant they included both Democrats and Republicans. Since both distracters are correct, the best answer to the question must be elsewhere.

   C is incorrect. The passage states that progressive reformers were mostly middle class, making this another correct distracter, and thus not the best answer.

2. Notice that the question asks about the cause of the problems and not the problems themselves.

   B is correct. Industrialization is the cause of the problems. All of the other answers identify problems and not the cause.

   A is incorrect. Slums are the result of industrialization not the cause of the problems.

   C is incorrect. Poverty is a problem not a cause.

   D is incorrect. Poor factory conditions are the result of industrialization not the cause of the problems.

3. The question asks for an action that the reformers probably did *not* undertake.

   B is correct. Since the achievement of world peace was not one of reformers' stated goals, you can assume that they did not take action on this front.

   A, C, and **D** are incorrect. Reforming government, promoting social welfare, and economic reform, including efforts to curb the power of big business, were all progressive goals.

20 STRATEGIES FOR TEST PREPARATION

STRATEGIES

Strategies for Test Preparation

Political Cartoons

Cartoonists who draw political cartoons use both words and art to express opinions about political issues.

❶ Try to figure out what the cartoon is about. Titles and captions may give clues.

❷ Use labels to help identify the people, places, and events represented in the cartoon.

❸ Note when and where the cartoon was published.

❹ Look for symbols— that is, people, places, or objects that stand for something else.

❺ The cartoonist often exaggerates the physical features of people and objects. This technique will give you clues as to how the cartoonist feels about the subject.

❻ Try to figure out the cartoonist's message and summarize it in a sentence.

World Cultures and Geography Sample

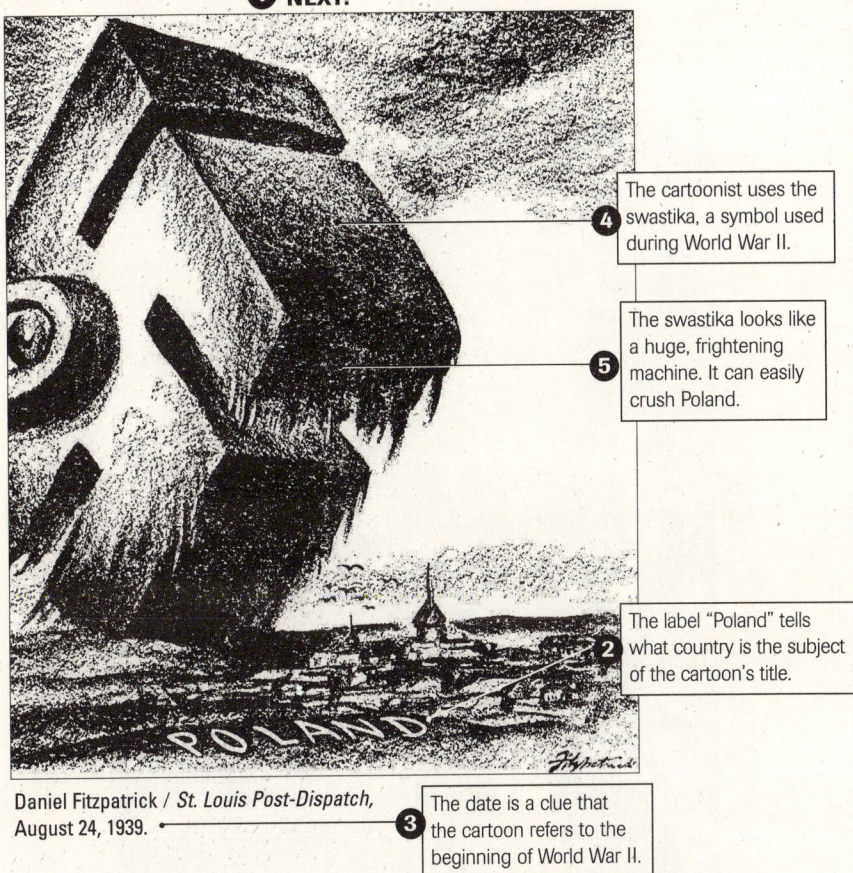

❶ "NEXT!"

❹ The cartoonist uses the swastika, a symbol used during World War II.

❺ The swastika looks like a huge, frightening machine. It can easily crush Poland.

❷ The label "Poland" tells what country is the subject of the cartoon's title.

Daniel Fitzpatrick / *St. Louis Post-Dispatch*, August 24, 1939.

❸ The date is a clue that the cartoon refers to the beginning of World War II.

1. What does the swastika in the cartoon stand for?

   A the Soviet Union
   B Nazi Germany
   C the Polish army
   D the Austrian military

❻ 2. Which sentence best summarizes the cartoonist's message?

   A Germany will attack Poland next.
   B Poland should stop Germany.
   C Germany will lose this battle.
   D Poland will fight a civil war.

answers: 1 (B), 2 (A)

Part 2 Test-Taking Strategies and Practice 21

Name _____ Date _____

PRACTICE

Strategies for Test Preparation

United States History Sample

Directions: This cartoon deals with the President Andrew Jackson and the actions he took during his administration. Use the cartoon and your knowledge of U.S. history to answer the questions below.

1. Why is President Jackson standing on torn papers labeled U.S. Constitution and U.S. Bank?

   A Jackson firmly supports both the Constitution and the Bank
   B Jackson is harming both the Constitution and the Bank.
   C Jackson wants the Constitution and the Bank to stand firm.
   D The Constitution and the Bank are commanded by Jackson.

2. Which statement summarizes the cartoonist view of President Jackson?

   A Jackson should become a king.
   B Jackson is a very strong leader
   C Jackson is dangerous because he tramples on the Constitution.
   D Jackson uses the veto power too often.

Name _____ Date _____

PRACTICE

Strategies for Test Preparation

World Cultures and Geography Sample

Directions: This cartoon deals with the fall of the Berlin Wall in 1989 and the beginning of the end of communism in Eastern Europe. Use the cartoon and your knowledge of world cultures and geography to answer the questions below.

Source: Jeff Koterba/Omaha World Herald

1 Which country does the dinosaur represent?

   A the Soviet Union
   B the United States
   C Great Britain
   D China

2 In the view of the cartoonist, the country represented here is

   A alive and doing well.
   B on its way to becoming extinct.
   C angry and terrifying.
   D big and dangerous.

Part 2 Test-Taking Strategies and Practice 23

ANSWERS

Strategies for Test Preparation

Thinking Through the Answers

Questions from Page 22:

1. **B** is correct. Jackson hated the bank and abuses his veto power in the Constitution to destroy the bank.

   A and **C** are incorrect. Jackson did not support the bank.
   D is incorrect. The Constitution is the law of the land, not the President.

2. **C** is correct. By showing Jackson as a king stepping on the Constitution, the cartoonist is suggesting that Jackson threatens a democratic way of life.

   A is incorrect. The cartoonist suggests presidents should not be thought of as kings.
   B is incorrect. The cartoonist shows Jackson as a king but does not indicate how powerful he is.
   D is incorrect. Jackson is shown with a veto in his hand but there is no way of knowing if he used it too often.

Questions from Page 23:

1. **A** is correct. You should recall that the hammer and sickle, which appears on the dinosaur, is the symbol of the Soviet Union. In addition, it is the Soviet Union that built the Berlin Wall, which is represented by the dinosaur's tail.

   B and **C** are incorrect. Neither of these answers is right for the reasons stated above.
   D is incorrect. While China is a Communist nation, it is not associated with either the hammer and sickle symbol or the Berlin Wall.

2. **B** is correct. By representing the country—the Soviet Union—as an extinct creature, the cartoonist feels that the Soviet Union and its Communist system will follow the way of the dinosaur and disappear.

   A is incorrect. Dinosaurs are extinct.
   C and **D** are incorrect. While dinosaurs can be all of these things, the cartoonist depicts this dinosaur in none of these ways—and thus most likely intends the creature to represent something else.

STRATEGIES

Strategies for Test Preparation

Charts

Charts present information in a visual form. History textbooks use several types of charts, including tables, flow charts, Venn diagrams, and concept webs. The type of chart most commonly found in standardized tests is the table. It organizes information in columns and rows for easy viewing.

❶ Read the title and identify the broad subject of the chart.

❷ Read the column and row headings and any other labels. This will provide more details about the subject of the chart.

❸ Compare and contrast the information from column to column and row to row.

❹ Try to draw conclusions from the information in the chart. Ask yourself: What trends does the chart show?

❺ Read the questions, and then study the chart again.

United States History Sample

Review difficult or unfamiliar words. Here, the term *nativity* means "place of birth."

❶ United States Population by Region and Nativity, 1890–1920

	1890	1900	1910	1920
Northeast				
Total Population	17,407,000	21,047,000	25,869,000	29,662,000
% Native Born	78	77	74	77
% Foreign Born	22	23	26	23
North Central				
Total Population	22,410,000	26,333,000	29,889,000	34,020,000
% Native Born	82	84	84	86
% Foreign Born	18	16	16	14
South				
Total Population	20,028,000	24,524,000	29,389,000	33,126,000
% Native Born	97	98	97	97
% Foreign Born	3	2	3	3
West				
Total Population	3,134,000	4,309,000	7,082,000	9,214,000
% Native Born	76	79	79	82
% Foreign Born	24	21	21	18

Source: *Historical Statistics of the United States*

❸ Compare changes in population over time and contrast statistics among regions.

1 The two regions with the highest percentage of foreign-born inhabitants are the

A Northeast and the West.
B West and the South.
C South and the North Central.
D North Central and the Northeast.

2 When did immigration to the Northeast peak?

A Between 1910 and 1920
B Before 1900
C Between 1900 and 1910
D After 1920

answers: 1 (A), 2 (C)

Name _____ Date _____

PRACTICE
Strategies for Test Preparation

United States History Sample

Directions: Use the chart and your knowledge of U.S. history to answer the questions below.

MAJOR CIVIL WAR BATTLES

Battle	Year	Place	Outcome	Significance
Bull Run (First)	1861	Virginia	Southern victory	showed South's resolve to fight
Antietam	1862	Maryland	Northern victory	bloodiest day of fighting in U.S. history
Seven Days'	1862	Virginia	Southern victory	saved Richmond from the Union
Gettysburg	1863	Pennsylvania	Northern victory	crushed all hopes for a Confederate victory in the North
Vicksburg	1863	Mississippi	Northern victory	split the South in two

1. Which stated was the site of the most major battles?

   A Virginia
   B Maryland
   C Mississippi
   D North Carolina

2. All of the following battles took place in Confederate territory EXCEPT

   A Bull Run.
   B Vicksburg.
   C Gettysburg.
   D Seven Days'.

3. Why is the battle at Gettysburg considered a turning point in the war?

   A Stonewall Jackson was killed there.
   B General Mead finally used the federal troops he commanded.
   C The forces of the South had their greatest victory.
   D The North crushed the South's chances of victory.

26 STRATEGIES FOR TEST PREPARATION

Name _____   Date _____

PRACTICE

Strategies for Test Preparation

World Cultures and Geography Sample

Directions: Use the chart and your knowledge of world cultures and geography to answer the questions below.

Country	1999	2025	2050
Belgium	10,182	9,533	7,609
Brazil	171,853	209,587	228,145
China	1,246,872	1,407,739	1,322,435
India	1,000,849	1,415,274	1,706,951
Japan	126,182	119,865	101,334
Nigeria	113,829	203,423	337,591
United States	272,640	335,360	394,241

Source: *The World Almanac and Book of Facts 2000*

1. Which country moved from second most populous to most populous between 1999 and 2050?

   A China
   B India
   C Brazil
   D United States

2. Which country's population decreased the most between 1999 and 2050?

   A India
   B Nigeria
   C Japan
   D Belgium

3. When will the population of India surpass that of China?

   A 1999
   B 2025
   C 2050
   D The chart does not give that information

Name _____ Date _____

ANSWERS

Strategies for Test Preparation

Thinking Through the Answers

Questions from Page 26:

1. **A** is correct. According to the chart, two battles took place in Virginia, more than any other state shown.

   B and **C** are incorrect. The chart indicates only one major battle in each of these states, making them both incorrect.

   D is incorrect. North Carolina does not appear on the chart, and thus cannot be the right answer.

2. To answer this question correctly, you need to recall which states on the chart did not belong to the Confederacy.

   C is correct. Pennsylvania, where the Battle of Gettysburg took place, was not a member of the Confederacy.

   A, B, and **D** are incorrect. Bull Run, Vicksburg, and the Seven Days' Battles took place in Confederate states.

3. Study the part of the chart labeled Significance. There you will see that Gettysburg is listed as a Northern victory that crushed the hopes of the South.

   D is correct.

   A, B, and **C** are incorrect. None of these answers are addressed in the chart.

Questions from Page 27:

1. **B** is correct. As the chart indicates, India was the second most populous country in 1999 and will be the most populous in 2050.

   A is incorrect. According to the chart, China dropped from most populous to second most populous during this time.

   C and **D** are incorrect. Neither of these countries was the second most populous country in 1999 or the most populous in 2050.

2. The question asks for the country whose population *decreased* the most.

   C is correct. According to the chart, Japan is the country whose population decreased the most during this time period.

   A and **B** are incorrect. These countries experienced the largest increases of the nations listed on the chart and thus neither are the right answer.

   D is incorrect. The population of Belgium decreased, but not as much as it did in Japan.

3. **B** is correct. Notice that in 2025 the population of India is higher than that of China.

   A is incorrect. At this time the population of China is higher than India.

   C is incorrect. India's population will have surpassed China's in 2025.

   D is incorrect. The answer can be determined from the information in the chart.

STRATEGIES

Strategies for Test Preparation

Line and Bar Graphs

Graphs show statistics in a visual form. Line graphs are particularly useful for showing changes over time. Bar graphs make it easy to compare numbers or sets of numbers.

❶ Read the title and identify the broad subject of the graph.

❷ Study the labels on the vertical and horizontal axes to see the kinds of information presented in the graph. Note the intervals between amounts and between dates. This will help you read the graph more efficiently.

❸ Look at the source line and evaluate the reliability of the information in the graph. Government statistics on education tend to be reliable.

❹ Study the information in the graph and note any trends.

❺ Draw conclusions and make generalizations based on these trends.

❻ Read the questions carefully, and then study the graph again.

United States History Sample

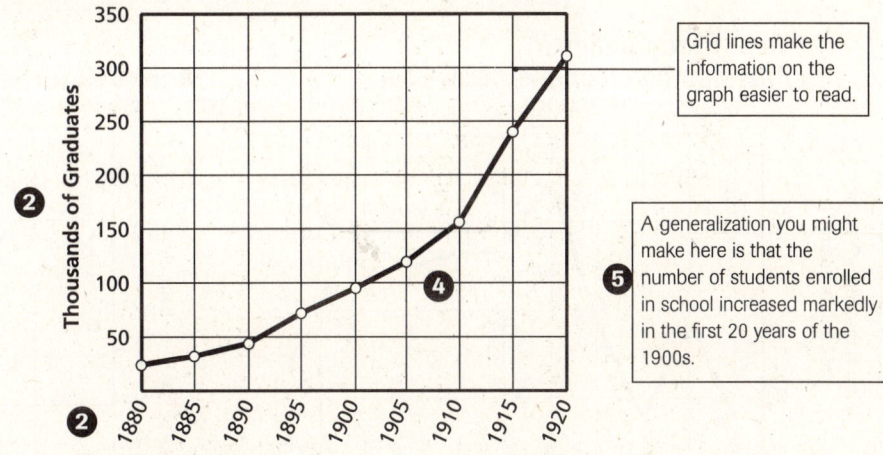

❻ 1 How many students graduated from high school in 1905?

A Exactly 100,000
B About 125,000
C About 150,000
D Exactly 175,000

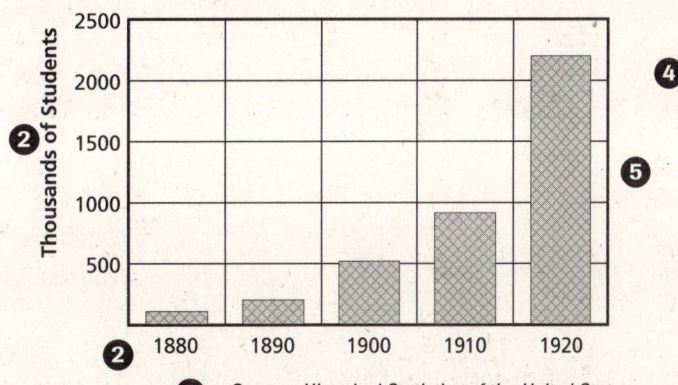

❻ 2 Which one of the following sentences do you think best describes the trend shown in the bar graph?

A The number of students enrolled steadily increased.
B The number of students enrolled showed little change.
C The number of students enrolled rose and fell.
D The number of students enrolled steadily decreased.

answers: 1 (B), 2 (A)

Part 2 Test-Taking Strategies and Practice **29**

Name _____ Date _____

PRACTICE
Strategies for Test Preparation

United States History Sample

Directions: Use the graphs and your knowledge of U.S. history to answer the questions below.

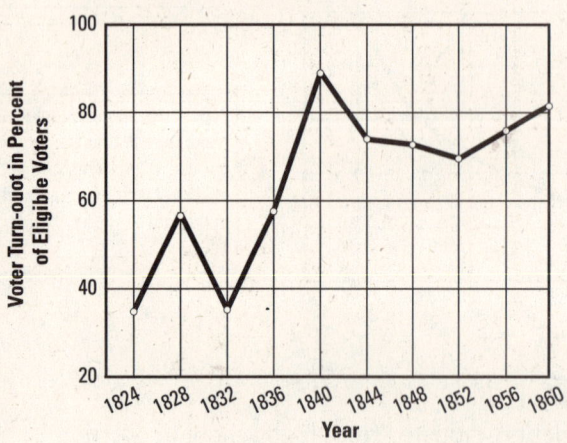

Voter Participation in Presidential Elections, 1824–1860

Source: *Historical Statistics of the United States: Colonial Times to 1970*

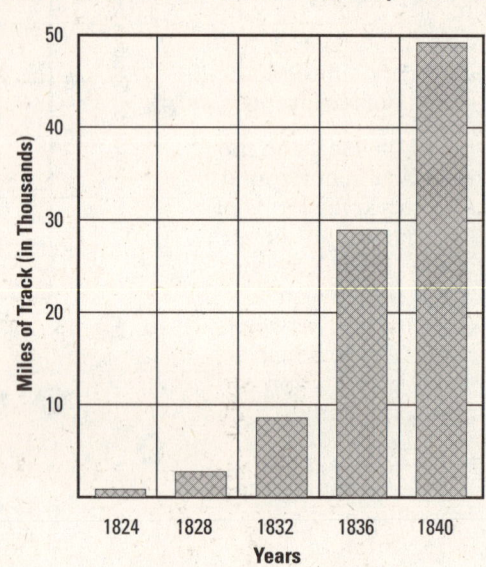

Miles of Railroad Tracks in U.S., 1850–1870

Source: *Historical Statistics of the United States: Colonial Times to 1970*

1. In which year was voter participation at about 80 percent?

   A 1832
   B 1848
   C 1852
   D 1860

2. Voter participation increased between all of the following years EXCEPT

   A 1824–1828.
   B 1836–1840.
   C 1848–1852.
   D 1856–1860.

3. Approximately how many miles of track had been constructed by 1840?

   A 25,000
   B 35,000
   C 45,000
   D 50,000

4. About eight thousand miles of track had been built by

   A 1824.
   B 1828.
   C 1832.
   D 1836.

30 STRATEGIES FOR TEST PREPARATION

Name _____   Date _____

PRACTICE — Strategies for Test Preparation

World Cultures and Geography Sample

Directions: Use the graphs and your knowledge of world cultures and geography to answer the questions below.

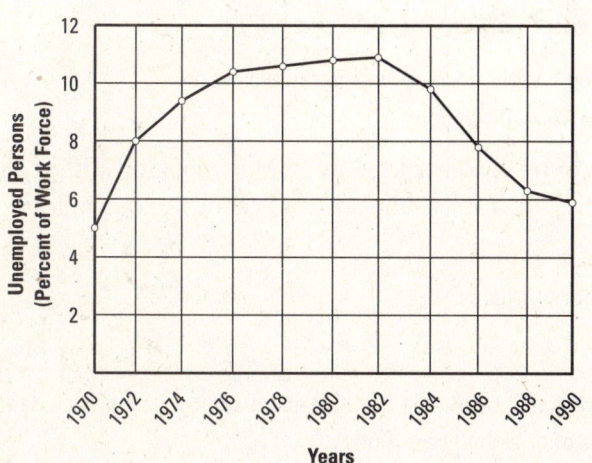

Unemployment in Great Britain, 1970–1990

Source: B.R. Mitchell, *International Historical Statistics: Europe 1750–1993*

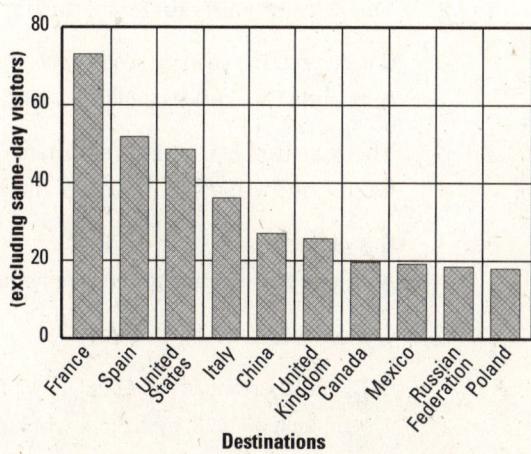

World's Top 10 Tourist Destinations, 1999

Source: World Tourism Organization as found in *The World Almanac and Book of Facts 2001*

1. The year that Great Britain showed its first decline in unemployment was
   A 1974.
   B 1978.
   C 1980.
   D 1984.

2. Which statement describes the information about unemployment in Great Britain presented in the graph?
   A Unemployment stayed high throughout the 1970s.
   B Unemployment rose in the 1970s and then fell in the 1980s.
   C A change in government policies brought unemployment down in the 1980s.
   D Unemployment stayed the same throughout the period.

3. The country that welcomed roughly as many tourists as China was
   A France.
   B Spain.
   C Italy.
   D the United States.

4. Which continent had the greatest number of visitors?
   A Europe
   B Asia
   C North America
   D Africa

Part 2 Test-Taking Strategies and Practice

ANSWERS

Strategies for Test Preparation

Thinking Through the Answers

Questions from Page 30:

1 **D** is the correct answer. The vote in 1860 was about 80 percent.

   A, B, and **C** are incorrect. The percentages shown for these years are under 80 percent.

2 The question asks for years during which voter participation decreased.

   C is correct. The years between 1848-1852 showed a slight decrease in voter participation.
   A, B, and **D** are incorrect. All show increases in voter participation.

3 The question asks for an estimate of miles of track constructed by 1840. By looking at the height of the bar for the 1840 and the y axis, you can see the answer is about 50,000 miles.

   D is correct.
   A, B, and **C** are incorrect. They are not accurate for the 1840s.

4 **C** is correct.

   B, C, and **D** are incorrect. About 1,000 miles of track had been built by 1824; about 2,500 miles of track had been built by 1828; by 1836 nearly 28,000 miles of track had been built.

Questions from Page 31:

1 The question asks for the first year there was a *decline* in unemployment.

   D is correct. The first year unemployment dropped was 1984.
   A is incorrect. 1974 was a year of increasing unemployment.
   B is incorrect. Unemployment in 1978 was increasing.
   C is incorrect. By 1980, unemployment in Great Britain was peaking.

2 **B** is correct. The graph shows an increase and then a decrease in unemployment in the 1970s and 1980s.

   A and **D** are not correct. The graph shows a decrease in unemployment in the 1980s.
   C is not correct. The graph gives no indication as to why unemployment decreased.

3 **B** is correct. With nearly 54 million tourists, Spain roughly doubled the number of tourists visiting China.

   A is incorrect. With 73 million tourists in 1999, France had closer to three times the number of tourists to China.
   C and **D** are incorrect. As the graph indicates, Spain has closer to twice as many tourists as China than either of these two countries.

4 To answer the question you need to recall that France, Spain, Italy, and the United Kingdom are located in Europe.

   A is correct.
   B, C, and **D** are incorrect. Only China is located in Asia, only the United States in North America, and no country is listed for Africa.

32 STRATEGIES FOR TEST PREPARATION

STRATEGIES

Strategies for Test Preparation

Pie Graphs

A pie, or circle, graph shows the relationship among parts of a whole. These parts look like slices of a pie. Each slice is shown as a percent of the whole pie.

❶ Read the title of the chart to find out what information is represented.

❷ The graph may provide a legend, or key, that tells you what different slices represent.

❸ The size of the slice is related to the percentage. The larger the percentage, the larger the slice.

❹ Look at the source line that tells where the graph is from. Ask yourself if you can depend on this source to provide reliable information.

❺ Read the questions carefully, and study the graph again.

World Cultures and Geography Sample

❶ **World Population by Region, 2000**

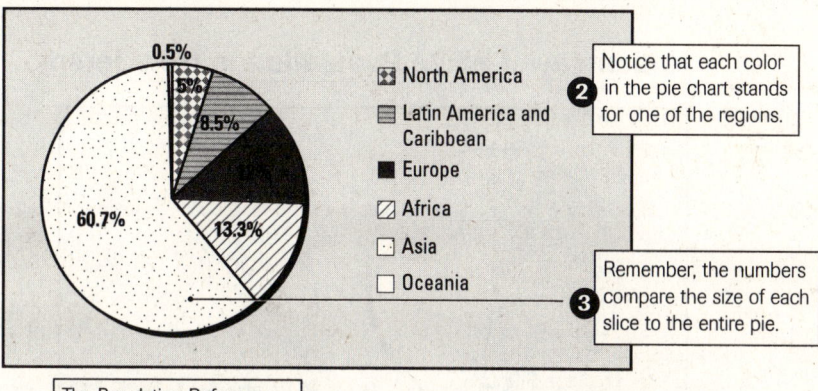

Pie chart showing:
- 0.5%
- 5%
- 8.5%
- 60.7%
- 13.3%

Legend:
- North America
- Latin America and Caribbean
- Europe
- Africa
- Asia
- Oceania

❷ Notice that each color in the pie chart stands for one of the regions.

❸ Remember, the numbers compare the size of each slice to the entire pie.

❹ **Source:** Population Reference Bureau

The Population Reference Bureau studies population data for the United States and other countries.

❺ **1** Which region accounts for nearly two-thirds of the world's population?

A Africa
B North America
C Europe
D Asia

2 Two regions have nearly the same percentage of the world's population. They are

A Africa; Latin America and Caribbean.
B Europe; Africa.
C Latin America and Caribbean; Europe.
D North America; Europe.

To answer this question, find the two percentages in the pie graph that are almost the same.

answers: 1 (D), 2 (G)

Name _____   Date _____

PRACTICE   Strategies for Test Preparation

United States History Sample

Directions: Use the pie graph and your knowledge of U.S. history to answer the questions below.

Nationality of White Population in New Jersey

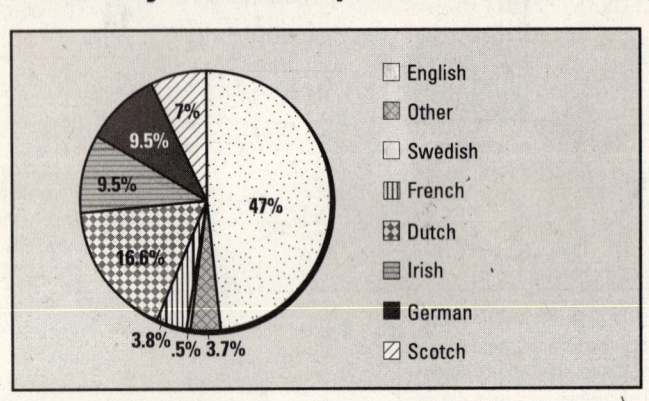

- English
- Other
- Swedish
- French
- Dutch
- Irish
- German
- Scotch

Percentages shown: 47%, 16.6%, 9.5%, 9.5%, 7%, 3.8%, .5%, 3.7%

Source: *Historical Statistics of the United States*

1. The nationality that accounts for the second largest percentage of New Jersey's population is
   A English.
   B Dutch.
   C Irish.
   D German.

2. The two nationalities that are almost equally represented in New Jersey are the Irish and
   A Dutch.
   B English.
   C Germans.
   D Scotch.

3. The majority of the population in New Jersey can trace its roots to which continent?
   A Africa
   B Asia
   C South America
   D Europe

34 STRATEGIES FOR TEST PREPARATION

PRACTICE

Strategies for Test Preparation

World Culture and Geography Sample

Directions: Use the pie graph and your knowledge of world cultures and geography to answer the questions below.

The World's Refugees by Region

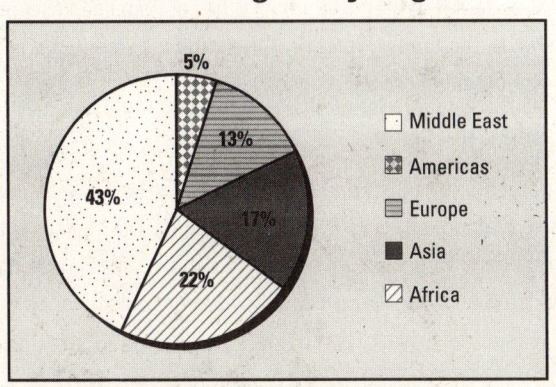

- Middle East: 43%
- Americas: 5%
- Europe: 13%
- Asia: 17%
- Africa: 22%

Source: *The World Almanac and Book of Facts 2000*

1. The region that ranks fourth in the number of refugees is

   A Africa.
   B Asia.
   C Europe.
   D the Middle East.

2. Africans seeking refuge in the Americas would have to travel across the

   A Indian Ocean.
   B Atlantic Ocean.
   C English Channel.
   D Mediterranean Sea.

3. What might be the reason for the great number of refugees from the Middle East?

   A They are seeking economic opportunities.
   B They are fleeing war or conflict in their homeland.
   C They want more land.
   D All of the above

Part 2 Test-Taking Strategies and Practice **35**

ANSWERS

Strategies for Test Preparation

Thinking Through the Answers

Questions from Page 34:

1. First look at the percentages listed on the pie and put them in order. The question asks for the second largest percentage.

    B is correct. The percentage of Dutch in New Jersey is greater than all other nationalities except the English.
    A, C, and **D** are incorrect. As the graph shows, the English represent the largest percentage, and the Irish and Germans are the third and fourth highest percentages respectively.

2. Look for two percentages that are almost the same.

    C is correct. As the graph indicates, the percentage of Irish and Germans in New Jersey is almost identical.
    A and **B** are incorrect. As the graph shows, the percentage of Dutch residents in New Jersey is almost twice the percentage of Irish, while the percentage of English residents is almost five times as great.
    D is incorrect. While the percentages of Scotch and Irish are similar, they are not as similar as the percentages of Germans and Irish.

3. Look at the countries listed in the pie graph. All of them are found in Europe.

    D is correct.
    A, B, and **C** are incorrect. There are no countries listed from these continents.

Questions from Page 35:

1. First look at the percentages listed on the pie and put them in order. The question asks for the fourth ranked percentage.

    C is correct. As the graph indicates, Europe has the fourth highest percentage of refugees behind the Middle East, Africa, and Asia.
    A, B, and **D** are incorrect. According to the graph, Africa and Asia rank second and third respectively, and the Middle East has the greatest number of refugees.

2. Think about the location of the Americas and Africa.

    B is the correct answer. The Atlantic Ocean is the main body of water separating Africa and the Americas, and thus must be crossed.
    A is incorrect. To reach the Americas from Africa by way of the Indian Ocean, one would have to cross both it and the Pacific Ocean.
    C and **D** are incorrect. Neither of these bodies of water leads directly to the Americas, and thus neither is the right answer.

3. Because the chart does not show reasons for the refugees leaving their lands, you must think about why people are considered refugees and not just immigrants.

    B is correct. Refugees often leave lands where conflict or war is taking place. There are many conflicts taking place in the Middle East.
    A and **C** are incorrect. These may be reasons for immigration, but not for refugee status.
    D is incorrect.

STRATEGIES

Strategies for Test Preparation

Physical Maps

Political maps show the divisions within countries. A country may be divided into states, provinces, etc. The maps also show where major cities are. They may also show mountains, oceans, seas, lakes, and rivers.

① Read the title of the map. This will give you the subject and purpose of the map.

② Read the labels on the map. They also give information about the map's subject and purpose.

③ Study the key or legend to help you understand the symbols in the map.

④ Use the scale to estimate distances between places shown on the map. Maps usually show the distance in both miles and kilometers.

⑤ Use the North arrow to figure out the direction of places on the map.

⑥ Read the questions. Carefully study the map to find the answers.

World Cultures and Geography Sample

① Canada and Its Provinces

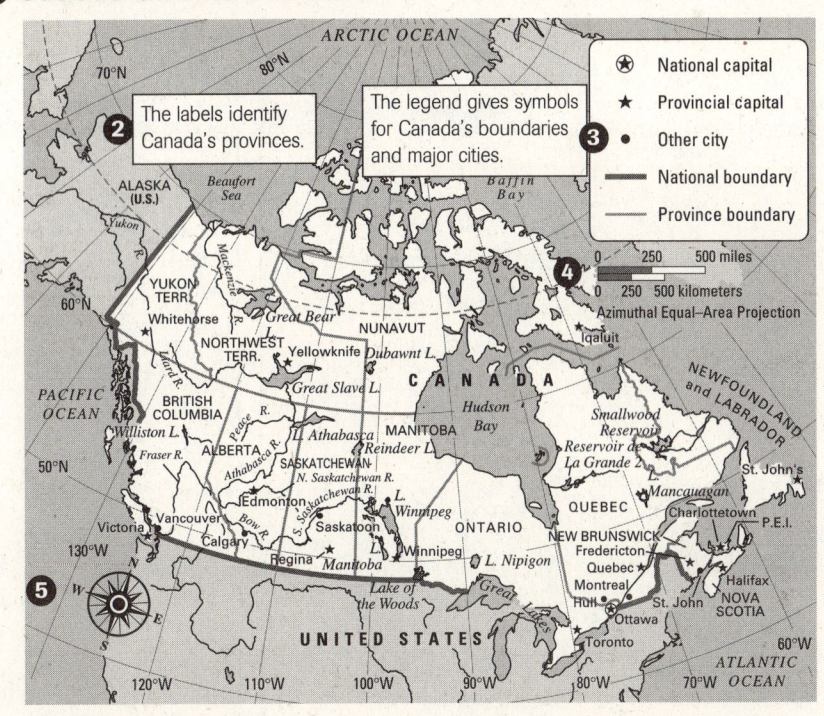

② The labels identify Canada's provinces.

③ The legend gives symbols for Canada's boundaries and major cities.

1. What province or territory is the farthest west?

   A Northwest Territories
   B Yukon Territory
   C British Columbia
   D Alberta

2. About how many miles is the United States-Canada border from the Great Lakes to the Pacific Ocean?

   A 1,000
   B 1,500
   C 2,000
   D 2,500

answers: 1 (B), 2 (B)

Part 2 Test-Taking Strategies and Practice 37

PRACTICE

Strategies for Test Preparation

United States History Sample

Directions: Use the map and your knowledge of United States and World history to answer the questions below.

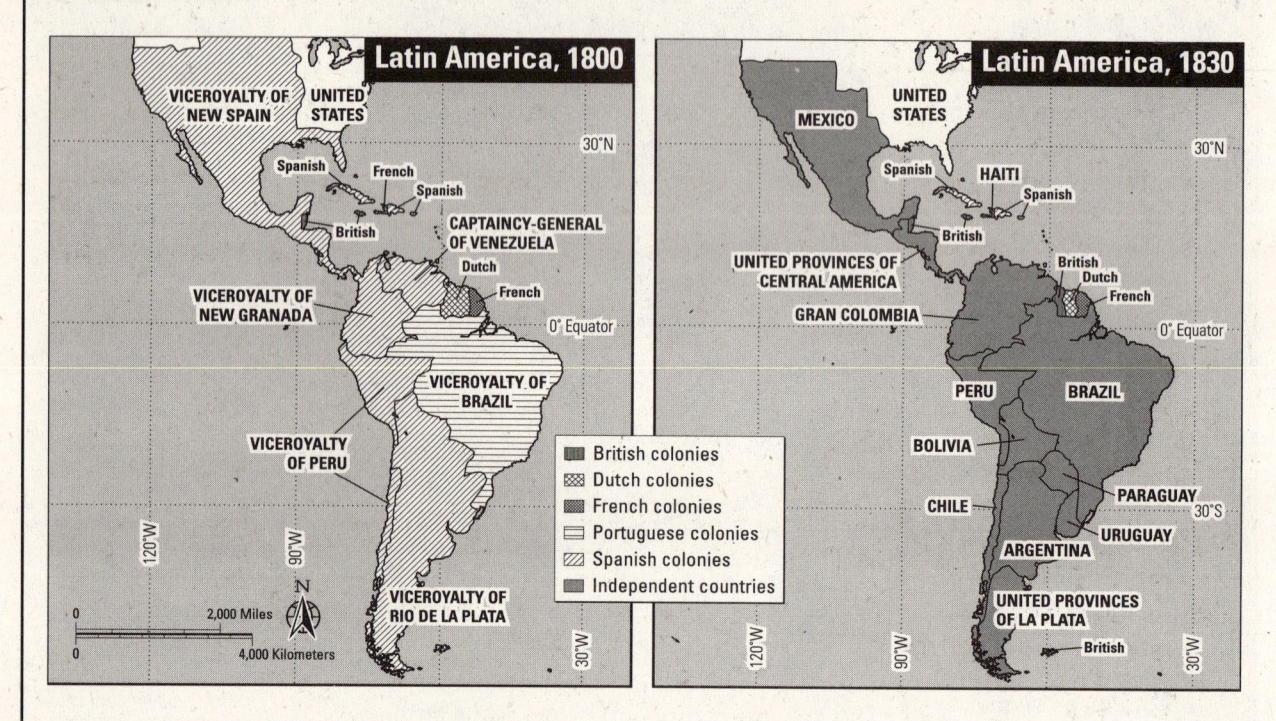

Latin America, 1800 — map showing Viceroyalty of New Spain, United States, Spanish, French, British, Dutch holdings, Captaincy-General of Venezuela, Viceroyalty of New Granada, Viceroyalty of Brazil, Viceroyalty of Peru, Viceroyalty of Rio de la Plata.

Latin America, 1830 — map showing United States, Mexico, Spanish, Haiti, British, Dutch, French, United Provinces of Central America, Gran Colombia, Peru, Bolivia, Brazil, Chile, Paraguay, Uruguay, Argentina, United Provinces of La Plata, British.

Legend: British colonies, Dutch colonies, French colonies, Portuguese colonies, Spanish colonies, Independent countries.

1. Between 1800 and 1830, Great Britain

   A seized Brazil from the Portuguese.
   B lost the most colonies in Latin America.
   C gained colonies in Latin America.
   D seized the land to the west of the United States.

2. Between 1800 and 1830, the United States

   A increased in size.
   B decreased in size.
   C stayed the same size.
   D established its current boundaries.

38 STRATEGIES FOR TEST PREPARATION

Name _____ Date _____

PRACTICE   Strategies for Test Preparation

World Cultures and Geography Sample

Directions: Use the map and your knowledge of world cultures and geography to answer the questions below.

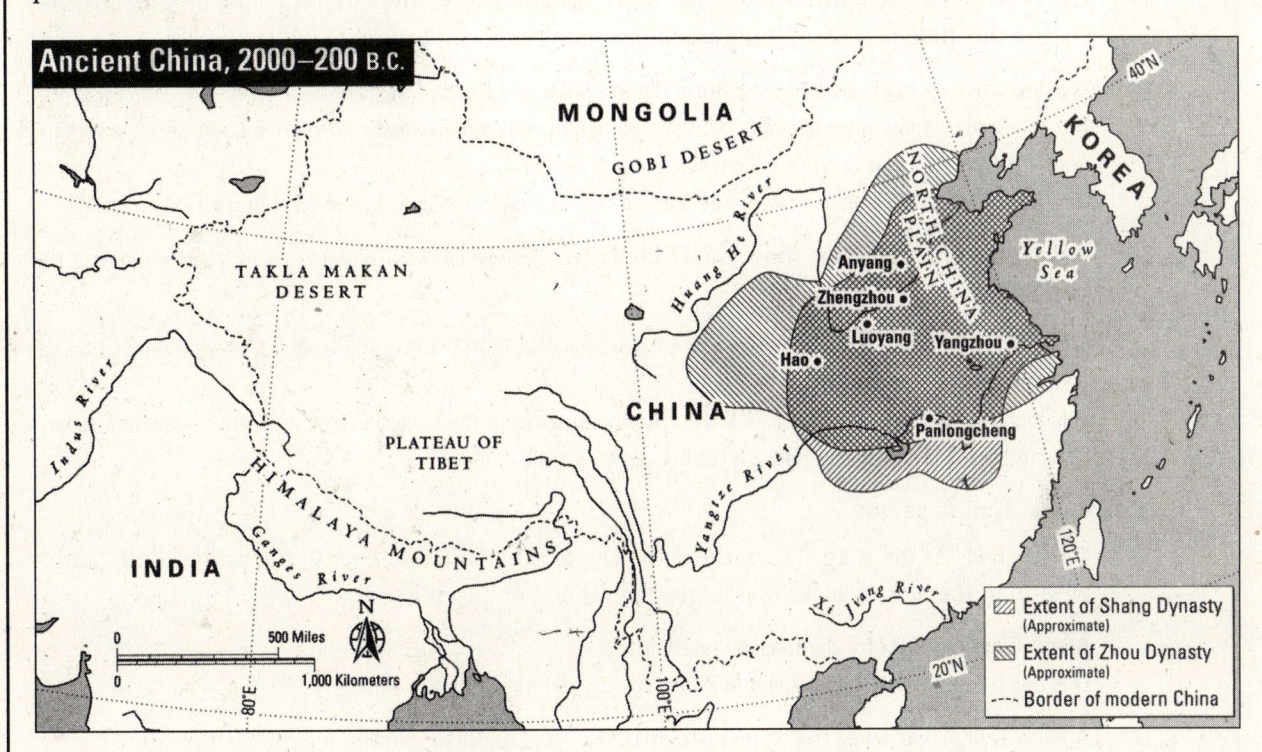

Ancient China, 2000–200 B.C.

[Map showing Ancient China with the extent of the Shang Dynasty and Zhou Dynasty, including labels for Mongolia, Gobi Desert, Takla Makan Desert, Plateau of Tibet, Himalaya Mountains, India, China, Korea, Yellow Sea, North China Plain, and cities Anyang, Zhengzhou, Luoyang, Hao, Yangzhou, and Panlongcheng. Rivers labeled include Indus River, Ganges River, Huang He River, Yangtze River, and Xi Jiang River.]

Legend:
- Extent of Shang Dynasty (Approximate)
- Extent of Zhou Dynasty (Approximate)
- Border of modern China

1. The extent of the Zhou Dynasty

   A was the same as the Shang Dynasty.
   B was smaller than the Shang Dynasty.
   C was larger than the Shang Dynasty.
   D reached the Korean peninsula.

2. The natural barrier that borders the northern edge of modern-day China is the

   A Gobi Desert.
   B Huang He River.
   C Himalaya Mountains.
   D Taklimakan Desert.

Part 2 Test-Taking Strategies and Practice 39

ANSWERS

Strategies for Test Preparation

Thinking Through the Answers

Questions from Page 38:

1 **C** is correct. As you can see from the maps, Britain is the only nation to actually gain colonies during this time period, as it occupied new lands without losing its old territories.

   A is incorrect. As the maps indicate, Brazil did not fall to the British but gained its independence.
   B is incorrect. As the maps show, Spain was the nation with the greatest presence in Latin America and thus was the country that lost the most colonies.
   D is incorrect. As the maps show, it was Mexico that occupied the land to the west of the United States.

2 **A** is correct. As the maps show, the United States increased its western boundaries during this period.

   B and **C** are incorrect. With the maps showing an increase in the size of the United States, neither of these distracters can be the right answer.
   D is incorrect. As you should recall, the current boundaries of the United States reach to the Pacific Ocean. As the maps indicate, this had not yet occurred by 1830.

Questions from Page 39:

1 **C** is correct. As the map shows, the Zhou Dynasty extended farther to the north, south, and west than the Shang, making it larger than the Shang Dynasty.

   A and **B** are incorrect for the reason stated above.
   D is incorrect. As the map shows, the Zhou Dynasty did not extend to Korea.

2 **A** is correct. To answer this question correctly, you need to use the legend to identify the borders of modern China. According to the map, the Gobi Desert sits to the north of modern-day China.

   B is incorrect. The Huang He River ran along the northern border of the Zhou empire, not modern-day China.
   C and **D** are incorrect. As the map indicates, the Himalaya Mountains run along the southern border of modern China, while the Taklimakan Desert stretches across China's western border.

STRATEGIES

Strategies for Test Preparation

Thematic Maps

Thematic maps focus on special topics. For example, a thematic map might show a country's natural resources or major battles in a war.

1 Read the title of the map. This will give you the subject and purpose of the map.

2 Read the labels on the map. They give information about the map's subject and purpose.

3 Study the key or legend to help you understand the symbols on the map. (The arrows show where Buddhism started and where it spread.)

4 Ask yourself whether the symbols show a pattern.

5 Read the questions. Carefully study the map to find the answers.

World Cultures and Geography Sample

1 The Spread of Buddhism

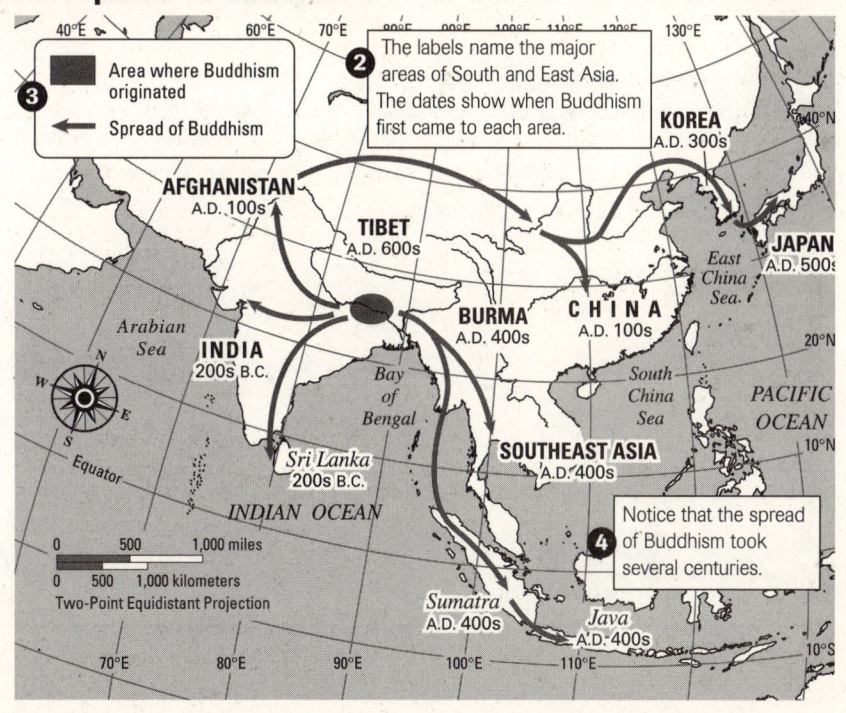

2 The labels name the major areas of South and East Asia. The dates show when Buddhism first came to each area.

3 Area where Buddhism originated / Spread of Buddhism

4 Notice that the spread of Buddhism took several centuries.

Map labels: AFGHANISTAN A.D. 100s; TIBET A.D. 600s; KOREA A.D. 300s; JAPAN A.D. 500s; BURMA A.D. 400s; CHINA A.D. 100s; INDIA 200s B.C.; Sri Lanka 200s B.C.; SOUTHEAST ASIA A.D. 400s; Sumatra A.D. 400s; Java A.D. 400s.

5

1. Where did Buddhism start?

   A Japan
   B India
   C Borneo
   D Afghanistan

2. Buddhism spread from China to

   A Japan and Tibet.
   B Tibet and Korea.
   C Korea and Japan.
   D All of the above

answers: 1 (B), 2 (C)

Part 2 Test-Taking Strategies and Practice

PRACTICE

Strategies for Test Preparation

United States History Sample

Directions: Use the map and your knowledge of U.S. history to answer the questions below.

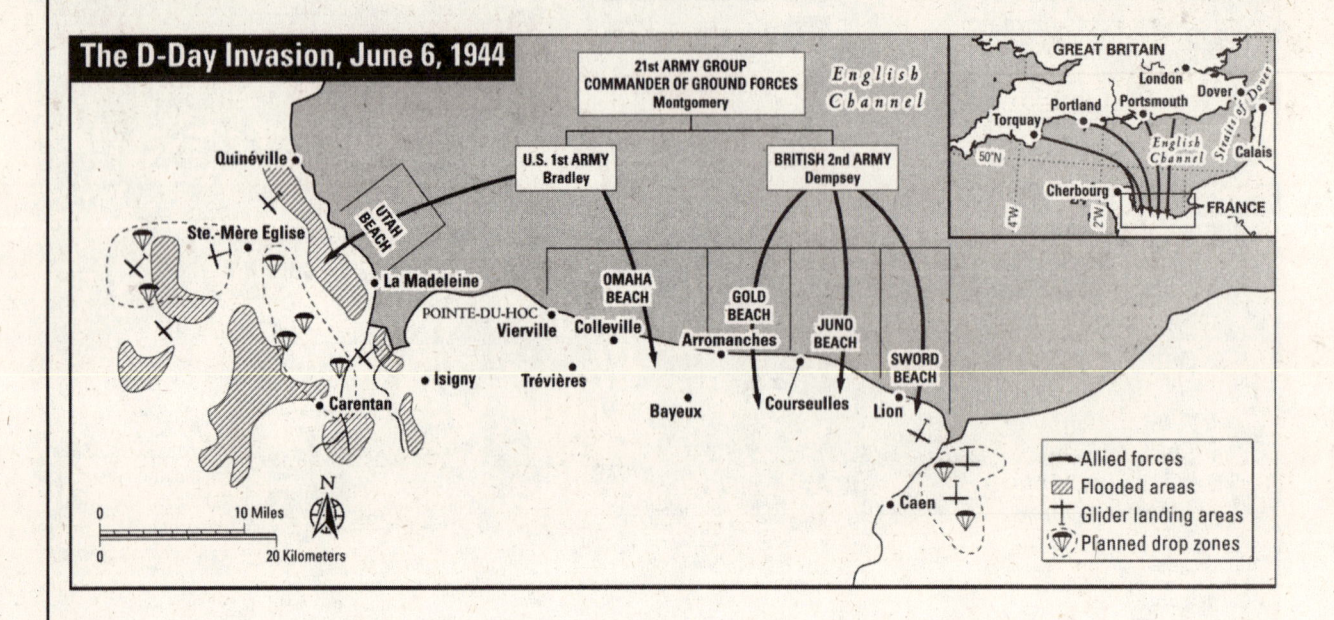

[Map: The D-Day Invasion, June 6, 1944]

1. The British 2nd Army was assigned to all the following beaches EXCEPT

   A Gold.
   B Juno.
   C Utah.
   D Caen.

2. Which of the following statements is accurate according to the map?

   A The town of Bayeux was close to a planned drop zone.
   B The entire D-Day invasion began from Portland, England.
   C The Allies crossed the English Channel at its narrowest point.
   D Ste.-Mère Eglise was close to both a glider landing area and planned drop zone.

PRACTICE

Strategies for Test Preparation

World Cultures and Geography Sample

Directions: Use the map and your knowledge of world cultures and geography to answer the questions below.

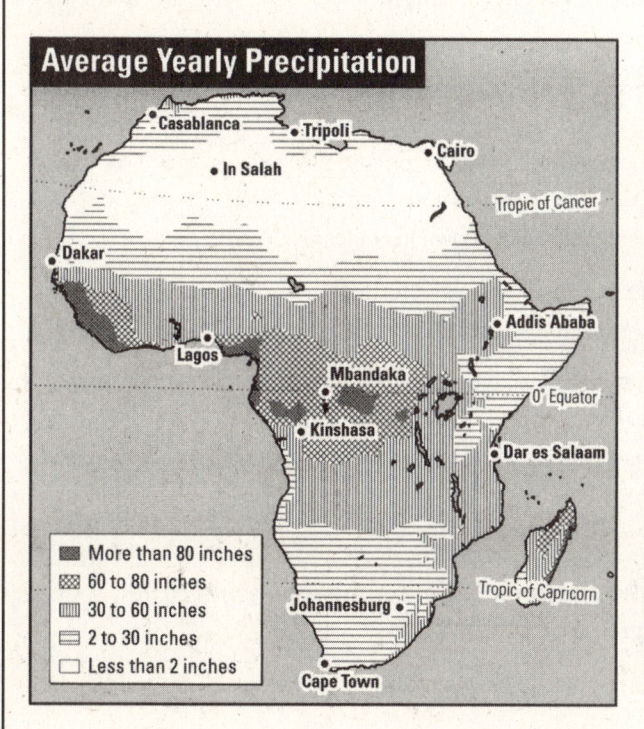

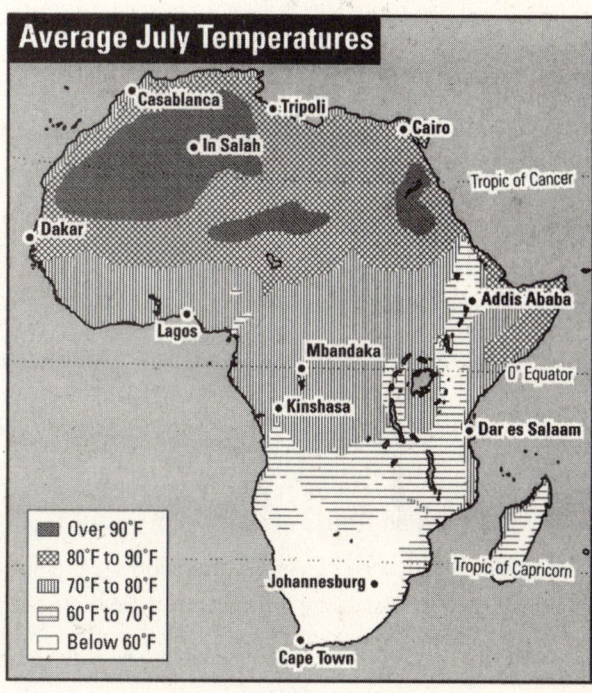

Average Yearly Precipitation

- More than 80 inches
- 60 to 80 inches
- 30 to 60 inches
- 2 to 30 inches
- Less than 2 inches

Average July Temperatures

- Over 90°F
- 80°F to 90°F
- 70°F to 80°F
- 60°F to 70°F
- Below 60°F

1. The coolest July temperatures in Africa are generally located in the

   A North.
   B South.
   C East.
   D West.

2. Based on the precipitation map, one could conclude that a large part of northern Africa was

   A rainforest.
   B farmland.
   C desert.
   D urbanized.

Part 2 Test-Taking Strategies and Practice 43

ANSWERS

Strategies for Test Preparation

Thinking Through the Answers

Questions from Page 42:

1. The question asks for the beach where the British 2nd Army was not assigned. Study the map to locate the British army assignments.

   C is correct. As the map indicates, it was the armed forces of the United States, not Britain, who fought on Utah Beach.

   A and **B** are incorrect. As the map shows, the British were assigned to these two beaches, and thus neither answer is correct.

   D is incorrect. As the map shows, Caen was not a beach but a town in France.

2. **D** is correct. The map shows that Ste.-Mère Eglise was close to both a glider landing area and planned drop zone.

   A is incorrect. As the map indicates, there were no planned drop zones near Bayeux.

   B is incorrect. As the inset map shows, the invasion began from several cities in England.

   C is incorrect. The inset map also indicates that the Allies did not cross the narrowest point of the channel, the Straits of Dover.

Questions from Page 43:

1. **B** is correct. As the map shows, the southern region of Africa is the continent's coolest spot with average temperatures below 60 degrees.

   A is incorrect. According to the map, the North is home to the warmest July temperatures, and thus it cannot be the right answer.

   C and **D** are incorrect. The map shows that average temperatures in these two regions are higher than they are in the South.

2. **C** is correct. Due to the region's lack of rain, it is more likely to be home to a desert than to rainforests or farmland.

   A and **B** are incorrect. Because rainforests and farmlands require a significant amount of rain, they probably could not be found in a region that receives less than 2 inches of rainfall annually.

   D is incorrect. It is impossible to tell from the map whether or not northern Africa contained numerous cities.

STRATEGIES

Strategies for Test Preparation

Time Lines

A time line is a type of chart that lists events in the order in which they occurred. In other words, time lines are a visual method of showing what happened when.

❶ Read the title to discover the subject of the time line.

❷ Identify the time period covered by the time line by noting the earliest and latest dates shown. On vertical time lines, the earliest date is shown at the top. On horizontal time lines, it is on the far left.

❸ Read the events and their dates in sequence. Notice the intervals between events.

❹ Use your knowledge of history to develop a fuller picture of the events listed in the time line. For example, you might try to identify some of the leading individuals involved in the events.

❺ Note how events are related to one another. Look particularly for cause-effect relationships.

❻ Use the information you have gathered from the above strategies to answer the questions.

United States History Sample

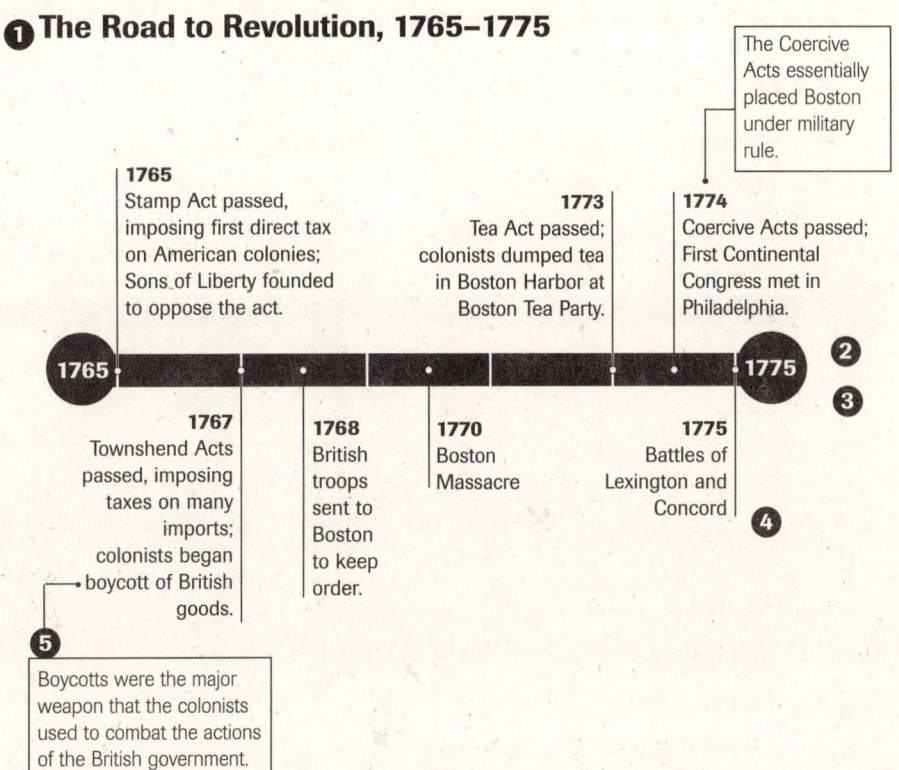

❶ The Road to Revolution, 1765–1775

The Coercive Acts essentially placed Boston under military rule.

1765 Stamp Act passed, imposing first direct tax on American colonies; Sons of Liberty founded to oppose the act.

1767 Townshend Acts passed, imposing taxes on many imports; colonists began boycott of British goods.

1768 British troops sent to Boston to keep order.

1770 Boston Massacre

1773 Tea Act passed; colonists dumped tea in Boston Harbor at Boston Tea Party.

1774 Coercive Acts passed; First Continental Congress met in Philadelphia.

1775 Battles of Lexington and Concord

❺ *Boycotts were the major weapon that the colonists used to combat the actions of the British government.*

1 How did the colonists respond to the passage of the Townshend Acts?

A They founded the Sons of Liberty.
B They dumped British tea in Boston Harbor.
C They began a boycott of British goods.
D They called the First Continental Congress.

2 About how much time passed between the Coercive Acts and the first battles of the Revolutionary War?

A One year
B Three years
C Seven years
D Nine years

answers: 1 (C), 2(A)

Part 2 Test-Taking Strategies and Practice **45**

PRACTICE

Strategies for Test Preparation

United States History Sample

Directions: Use the time line and your knowledge of U.S. history to answer the questions below.

America Becomes a World Power

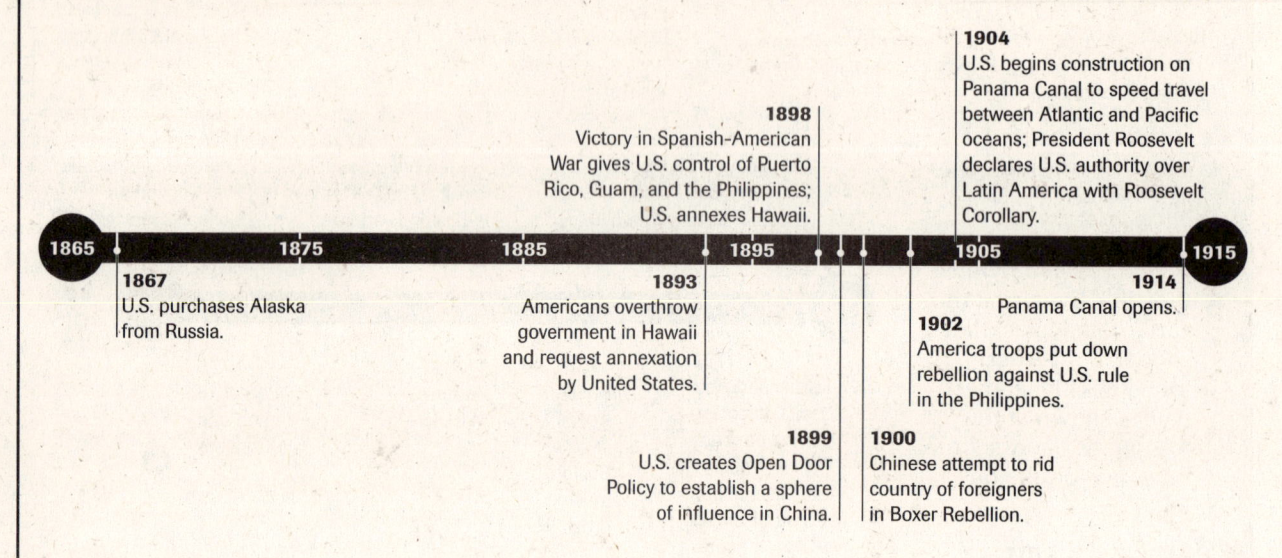

- **1865**
- **1867** U.S. purchases Alaska from Russia.
- **1893** Americans overthrow government in Hawaii and request annexation by United States.
- **1898** Victory in Spanish-American War gives U.S. control of Puerto Rico, Guam, and the Philippines; U.S. annexes Hawaii.
- **1899** U.S. creates Open Door Policy to establish a sphere of influence in China.
- **1900** Chinese attempt to rid country of foreigners in Boxer Rebellion.
- **1902** America troops put down rebellion against U.S. rule in the Philippines.
- **1904** U.S. begins construction on Panama Canal to speed travel between Atlantic and Pacific oceans; President Roosevelt declares U.S. authority over Latin America with Roosevelt Corollary.
- **1914** Panama Canal opens.
- **1915**

1 How long did it take to build the Panama Canal?

  A ten years
  B twelve years
  C fifteen years
  D cannot be determined

2 In what year did the United States add greatly to the lands it controlled?

  A 1885
  B 1893
  C 1898
  D 1904

3 Based on the time line, which of the following statements is NOT accurate?

  A Hawaii was not annexed right away after coming under U.S. control.
  B The United States met no resistance in its growth as a world power.
  C The Spanish-American War increased the number of U.S. territories.
  D The Panama Canal sped ocean travel between New York and Los Angeles.

PRACTICE

Strategies for Test Preparation

World Cultures and Geography Sample

Directions: Use the time line and your knowledge of world cultures and geography to answer the questions below.

Arab-Israeli Conflicts

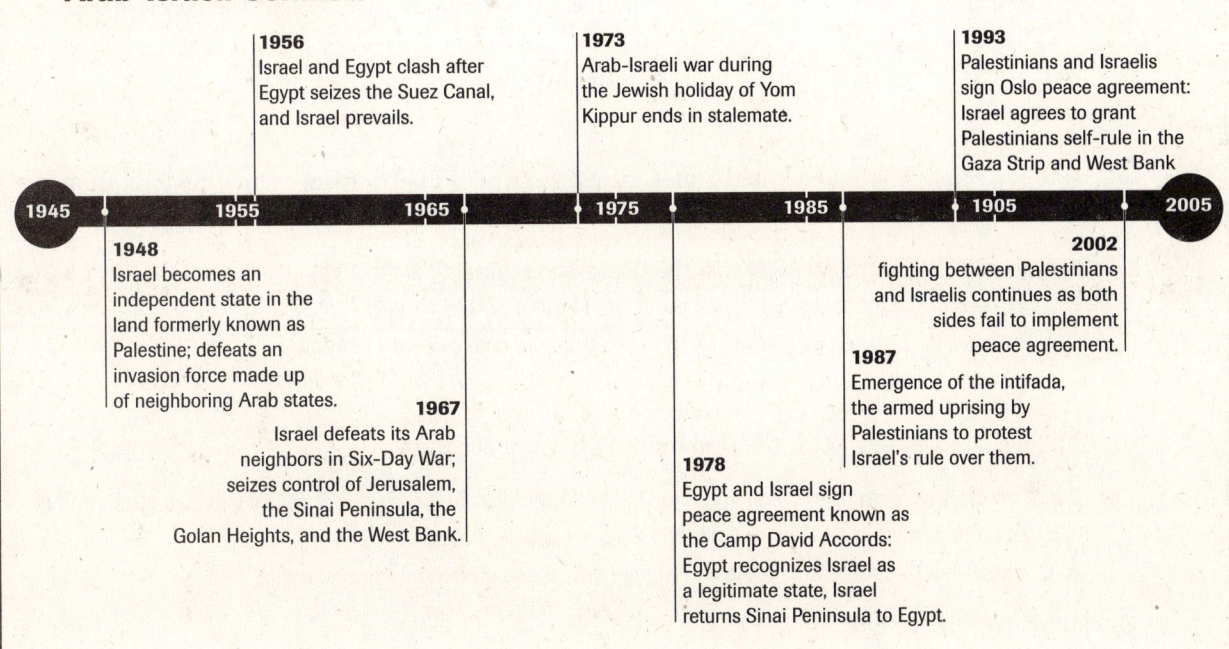

1956
Israel and Egypt clash after Egypt seizes the Suez Canal, and Israel prevails.

1973
Arab-Israeli war during the Jewish holiday of Yom Kippur ends in stalemate.

1993
Palestinians and Israelis sign Oslo peace agreement: Israel agrees to grant Palestinians self-rule in the Gaza Strip and West Bank

1945 — 1955 — 1965 — 1975 — 1985 — 1905 — 2005

1948
Israel becomes an independent state in the land formerly known as Palestine; defeats an invasion force made up of neighboring Arab states.

1967
Israel defeats its Arab neighbors in Six-Day War; seizes control of Jerusalem, the Sinai Peninsula, the Golan Heights, and the West Bank.

1978
Egypt and Israel sign peace agreement known as the Camp David Accords: Egypt recognizes Israel as a legitimate state, Israel returns Sinai Peninsula to Egypt.

1987
Emergence of the intifada, the armed uprising by Palestinians to protest Israel's rule over them.

2002
fighting between Palestinians and Israelis continues as both sides fail to implement peace agreement.

1. The years that witnessed a break in Arab-Israeli violence were 1978 and

    A 1956.
    B 1967.
    C 1987.
    D 1993.

2. Which peace agreements are listed on the time line?

    A Yom Kippur Agreement and Oslo Accords
    B Palestine Accords and Camp David Accords
    C Camp David Accords Oslo and Accords
    D Yom Kippur Agreement and Palestine Accords

3. Which of the following statements is accurate according to the time line?

    A Israel's current holdings include the Sinai Peninsula.
    B Israel and the Palestinians have yet to settle their dispute with each other.
    C Israel and its Arab neighbors have gone to war against each other only once.
    D It was several years after Israel became a state that the first Arab-Israeli fighting erupted.

Part 2 Test-Taking Strategies and Practice **47**

ANSWERS

Strategies for Test Preparation

Thinking Through the Answers

Questions from Page 46:

1 There is enough information on the time line to determine how long it took to build the canal.

   A is correct. According to the time line the construction on the canal began in 1904 and the canal opened in 1914—ten years later.

   B, C, and **D** are incorrect. These distracters are incorrect for the reason stated above.

2 **C** is correct. In 1898 the United States gained control of Puerto Rico, Guam, the Philippines and Hawaii.

   A is not correct. No land was gained by the United States government in 1885.
   B is not correct. No land was gained by the United States government in 1893.
   D is not correct. No land was gained by the United States government in 1904.

3 The question is asking for the statement that is not accurate.

   B is correct. According to the time line, the United States did meet resistance, as the Chinese attempted to expel them and other foreigners while the Filipinos rebelled against U.S. rule.

   A, C, and **D** are incorrect. According to the time line, these statements are accurate.

Questions from Page 47:

1 Look for years that mention peace activities.

   D is correct. The time line indicates it was during this year that the Israelis and Palestinians signed the Oslo peace agreement.

   A, C, and **D** are incorrect. Each of these years experienced violence or war.

2 **B** is correct. As the last entry in the time line indicates, the struggle between the Israelis and Palestinians continues.

   A is incorrect. Israel seized the Sinai Peninsula during the Six-Day War, but returned it to Egypt as a result of the Camp David Accords.

   C is incorrect. According to the time line, Israel and its Arab neighbors engaged in war on four separate occasions.

   D is incorrect. As the time line shows, the first Arab-Israeli war occurred the same year that Israel became a state.

STRATEGIES

Strategies for Test Preparation

Constructed Response

Constructed-response questions focus on a document, such as a photograph, cartoon, chart, graph, or time line. Instead of picking one answer from a set of choices, you write a short response. Sometimes, you can find the answer in the document. Other times, you will use what you already know about a subject to answer the question.

❶ Read the title of the document to get an idea of what it is about.

❷ Study the document.

❸ Read the questions carefully. Study the document again to find the answers.

❹ Write your answers. You don't need to use complete sentences unless the directions say so.

World Cultures and Geography Sample

❶ The Salt March

❷ This document is a photograph showing Mohandas K. Gandhi leading a demonstration.

Mohandas Gandhi and poet Sarojini Naidu lead Indians in a march down the west coast of India. They are protesting the Salt Acts of 1930.

1 Mohandas Gandhi was an important leader in what country?

❹ India

2 Read the title of the photograph. What was the Salt March?

It was a protest against the Salt Acts. These acts said that Indians could buy salt only from the British. They also had to pay sales taxes when they bought salt.

3 What principle did Gandhi follow to win independence for India? Describe the (ways) he put this principle into action.

❸ The question uses the plural "ways." Your answer must include more than one way.

passive resistance, civil disobedience, or nonviolence. He led peaceful marches against unjust laws. He organized boycotts of British goods. He also told people not to cooperate with the British government.

Part 2 Test-Taking Strategies and Practice **49**

PRACTICE

Strategies for Test Preparation

United States History Sample

Directions: Use the following graph and your knowledge of U.S. history to answer the questions below.

U.S. Slave Population, 1650–1750

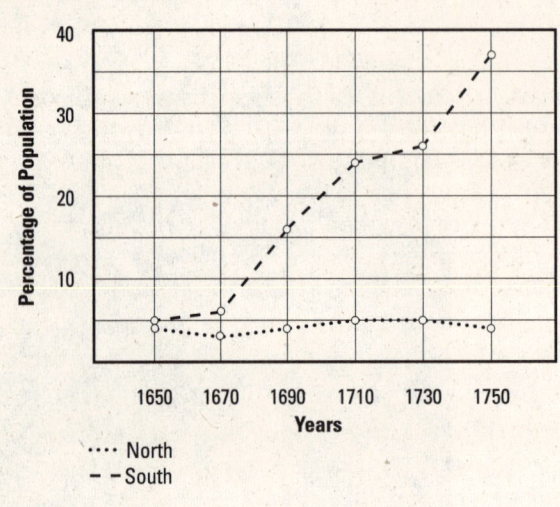

[Graph showing Percentage of Population (0–40) vs. Years (1650–1750), with North (dotted line) staying near 0, and South (dashed line) rising from near 0 in 1650 to about 37 in 1750.]

•••• North
– – South

Source: Fogel and Engerman, *Time on the Cross*, 1974

1. About what percentage of the South's total population did slaves account for by 1750?

2. What is the main idea of the graph?

3. What was the reason for the vast difference in the slave populations of the North and the South?

50 STRATEGIES FOR TEST PREPARATION

Name _____ Date _____

PRACTICE

Strategies for Test Preparation

World Cultures and Geography Sample

Directions: Read the following passage from one of the earliest Spanish missionaries in Mexico. Bernardinao de Sahagun describes Montezuma's encounter with the forces of Cortes. Use the passage and your knowledge of world cultures and geography to answer the questions. You do not need to use complete sentences.

> And as to their war gear, it was all iron. They were iron. Their headpieces were of iron. Their swords, their crossbows, their shields their lances were of iron.[4]
> The animals they rode—they looked like deer—were as high as roof tops.
>   They covered their bodies completely, all except their faces.
>   They were very white. Their eyes were like chalk. Their hair—on some it was yellow, on some it was black. They wore long beards; they were yellow, too. And there were some black-skinned ones with kinky hair.
>   What they ate was like what Aztecs ate during periods of fasting: it was large, it was white, it was lighter than tortilla; it was spongy like the inside of cornstalks; it tasted as if it had been made of flour of corn stalks; it was sweetish.
>
> —Bernardino de Sahagun in the *General History of the Things of New Spain*

[4] The Native Americans essentially had no metals. Aztec weapons were made of stone, and their minimal body armor and shields were made of fibers.

1. In what ways were the Spaniards physically different from the Aztec?

   _____
   _____
   _____

2. Sahagun describes a food eaten by the Spaniards. What is it?

   _____
   _____
   _____

3. Why might the Aztec leader Montezuma have been frightened by the description of the Spaniards?

   _____
   _____
   _____

Part 2 Test-Taking Strategies and Practice 51

ANSWERS

Strategies for Test Preparation

Thinking Through the Answers

Questions for Page 50:

1. about 37 percent

2. Slavery became widespread in the South but not in the North.

3. The South established a largely agricultural economy that relied greatly on slave labor, while the North developed an industrial economy that did not require the labor of slaves.

Questions for Page 51:

1. They were very white, had yellow or black hair, wore beards, and some were black-skinned with kinky hair.

2. bread

3. The strange animals and the war gear were very different from the Aztec and might be very dangerous.

STRATEGIES

Strategies for Test Preparation

Extended Response

Extended-response questions, like constructed-response questions, usually focus on one kind of document. However, they are more complex and require more time to complete than typical short-answer constructed-response questions. Some extended-response questions ask you to complete a chart, graph, or diagram. Still others ask you to write an essay, a report, or some other lengthier piece based on the document.

❶ Read the title of the document to get an idea of the subject.

❷ Study and analyze the document. Take notes on your ideas.

❸ Carefully read the extended-response questions. (Question 1 asks you to present the information in the chart in a time line. Question 2 asks you to write an essay by applying your knowledge of history to information in the chart.)

❹ If the question calls for some type of diagram, make a rough sketch on scrap paper first. Then, make a final copy of your diagram on the answer sheet.

❺ If the question requires an extended piece of writing, jot down ideas in outline form. Use this outline to write your answer.

United States History Sample

❶ Ratifying the Constitution

State	Date Ratified
Connecticut	January 9, 1788
Delaware	December 7, 1787
Georgia	January 2, 1788
Maryland	April 28, 1788
Massachusetts	February 6, 1788
New Hampshire	June 21, 1788
New Jersey	December 18, 1787
New York	July 26, 1788
North Carolina	November 21, 1789
Pennsylvania	December 12, 1787
Rhode Island	May 29, 1790
South Carolina	May 23, 1788
Virginia	June 25, 1788

❷

❸ 1. Use the information in the chart and your knowledge of U.S. history to create a time line for the ratification of the Constitution.

The Ratification of the Constitution

December 1787: Delaware became the first state to ratify, followed quickly by Pennsylvania and New Jersey.

January 1788: Georgia and Connecticut ratified.

February 1788: Massachusetts ratified.

April 1788: Maryland voted to ratify.

May 1788: South Carolina ratified.

June 1788: New Hampshire and Virginia voted to ratify. Constitution officially ratified.

July 1788: Influenced by Virginia's vote, New York ratified.

November 1789: North Carolina voted for ratification.

May 1790: Rhode Island made vote for ratification unanimous.

1787 — 1790

❹ For time lines and other diagrams, remember to include a title and all appropriate labels.

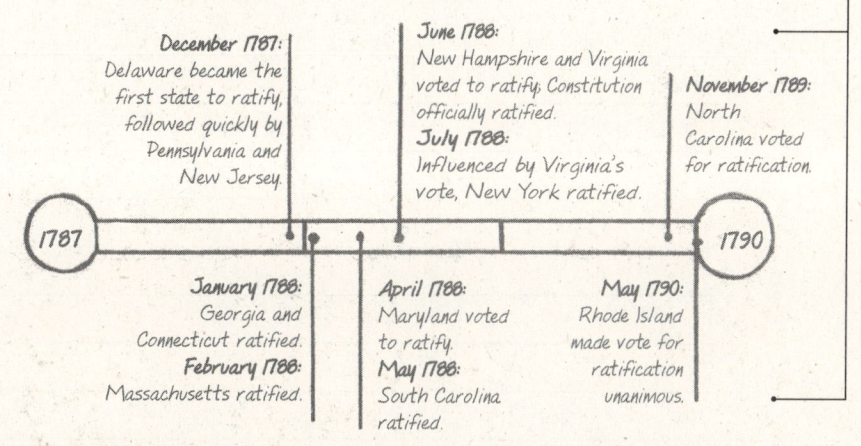

❸ 2. Write a brief essay explaining the significance of the Bill of Rights to the ratification of the Constitution.

❺ **Essay Rubric** The best essays will point out that the promise of a Bill of Rights was key to getting enough support to ensure ratification of the Constitution. The vote for ratification by Virginia—the largest of the states—was contingent upon the passage of a Bill of Rights.

Part 2 Test-Taking Strategies and Practice 53

Name _____   Date _____

PRACTICE
Strategies for Test Preparation

United States History Sample

Directions: Use the document and your knowledge of U.S. history to answer the questions below.

The Emancipation Proclamation

Two days after Lincoln appointed [Henry] Halleck general-in-chief, he made an equally significant shift in his policy toward slavery. . . . On July 13 [1862], riding in a carriage with Secretaries Seward and Welles to the funeral of [Edwin] Stanton's infant son, he informed these two conservative members of his cabinet that he "had about come to the conclusion that we must free the slaves or be ourselves subdued." Both Seward and Welles were startled, because hitherto [up until now] the President had been emphatic [forceful] in rejecting any proposal to have the national government interfere with slavery. Both said they needed more time to consider the idea. But the President urged them seriously to think about it, because "something must be done."

—From *Lincoln,* by David Herbert Donald

1 How did Lincoln's view of slavery change?

_____
_____
_____

2 In an essay, explain what the Emancipation Proclamation declared and its impact on slaves and on the Civil War itself.

_____
_____
_____
_____
_____
_____
_____
_____
_____
_____
_____
_____

Name _____   Date _____

PRACTICE
Strategies for Test Preparation

World Cultures and Geography Sample

Directions: Use the graph and your knowledge of world cultures and geography to answer the questions below.

Standing Armies*, Selected Countries

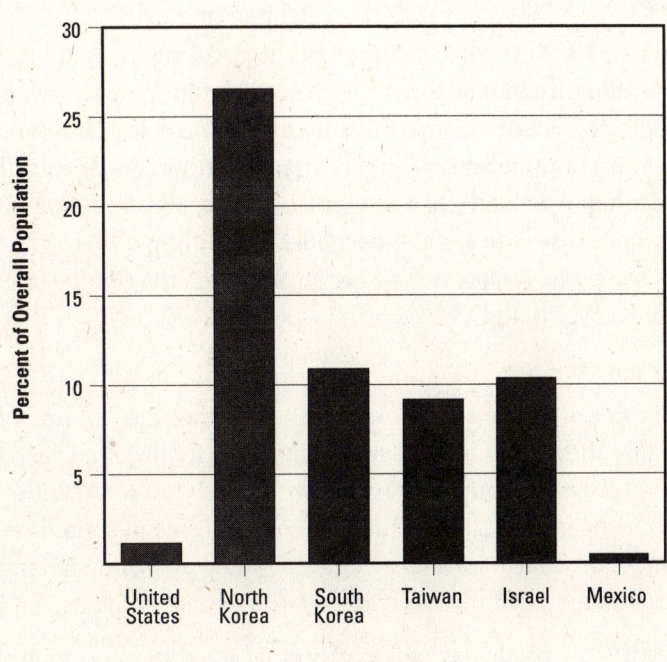

Bar graph showing Percent of Overall Population for:
- United States: ~1%
- North Korea: ~27%
- South Korea: ~11%
- Taiwan: ~9%
- Israel: ~10.5%
- Mexico: <1%

Countries

* includes active and reserve troops

Source: World Almanac Education Group, *The World Almanac and Book of Facts 2001*, Mahwah, NJ 2001, pp. 207, 800–854

1. What geographic and political factors might account for the large armies in North and South Korea, Taiwan, and Israel?

   _____
   _____
   _____

2. In an essay discuss what geographic and political features might contribute to the relatively small size of the U.S. army?

   _____
   _____
   _____

Part 2 Test-Taking Strategies and Practice 55

ANSWERS

Strategies for Test Preparation

Thinking Through the Answers

Questions from Page 54:

1. Lincoln had long thought that the federal government should not interfere with slavery where it already existed, but he eventually changed his mind and came to believe that it was the duty of the federal government to end slavery.

2. **ESSAY RUBRIC** The best essays will explain that the Emancipation Proclamation declared that all slaves under Confederate rule were free. The Proclamation had little effect on these slaves, since they were not under Union control. Nonetheless, the Proclamation had a tremendous impact on the war effort. For many Northerners, it gave the war a higher moral purpose by turning it into a fight against slavery. The Proclamation also intensified the war and made compromise between the two sides all but impossible. The South now realized that if it lost, its slave-based society would perish, and thus the Confederacy became more determined than ever to fight on.

Questions from Page 55:

1. North and South Korea share the same peninsula as well as a mutual hostility toward one another. Because they are neighbors and enemies, it follows that each would have a sizeable standing army. Taiwan's large army may have a good deal to do with the island's long-running hostility with its neighbor, China. China claims that Taiwan should be a part of China, but many Taiwanese disagree. Israel has a large standing army due in large part to its location next to several Arab states, most of which are sworn enemies of Israel.

2. **ESSAY RUBRIC** The best essay will explain that the relatively small size of the U.S. army may have to do with the fact that the United States is protected from invasion on both sides by vast oceans. Furthermore, the United States shares good relations with its neighbors to the north and south, Canada and Mexico. All of this makes the possibility of invasion fairly remote and thus lessens the need for a large army.

STRATEGIES

Strategies for Test Preparation

Document-Based Questions

To answer a document-based question, you have to study more than one document. First you answer questions about each document. Then you use those answers and information from the documents as well as your own knowledge of history to write an essay.

❶ Read the "Historical Context" section. It will give you an idea of the topic that will be covered in the question.

❷ Read the "Task" section carefully. It tells you what you will need to write about in your essay.

❸ Study each document. Think about the connection the documents have to the topic in the "Task" section.

❹ Read and answer the questions about each document. Think about how your answers connect to the "Task" section.

World Cultures and Geography Sample

Introduction

❶ Historical Context: For hundreds of years, Mongol nomads lived in different tribes. They sometimes fought among themselves. In the late 1100s, a new leader—Genghis Khan—united these tribes. He turned the Mongols into a powerful fighting army.

❷ Task: Discuss how the Mongols conquered Central and East Asia and how their rule affected Europeans' lives.

Part 1: Short Answer

Study each document carefully. Answer the questions that follow.

❸ Document 1: Mongol Warrior

❹ What were the characteristics of a Mongol Warrior?

The Mongols were great horsemen who could ride a long way without rest. They attacked without warning, and showed no mercy. They used clever tricks to frighten their enemies. Also, they borrowed or invented new weapons of war.

Part 2 Test-Taking Strategies and Practice 57

STRATEGIES

Strategies for Test Preparation

❺ Read the essay question carefully. Then write a brief outline for your essay.

❻ Write your essay. The first paragraph should introduce your topic. The middle paragraphs should explain it. The closing paragraph should restate the topic and your conclusion. Support your ideas with quotations or details from the documents. Add other supporting facts or details from your knowledge of world history.

❼ A good essay will contain the ideas in the rubric below.

❼ **Essay Rubric** The best essays will describe how the Mongols' tactics, fierce will, and strong military organization enabled them to conquer Central and East Asia. (Documents 1 and 2). The essays will also state that Mongol rule brought a period of peace and unity to regions that had been divided. This peace allowed trade to start again along the Silk Road (Document 2). This trade brought new ideas and products to Europe. Stories of the immense wealth in Mongol lands made Europeans want to tap into those riches (Document 3).

Document 2: The Mongol Empire

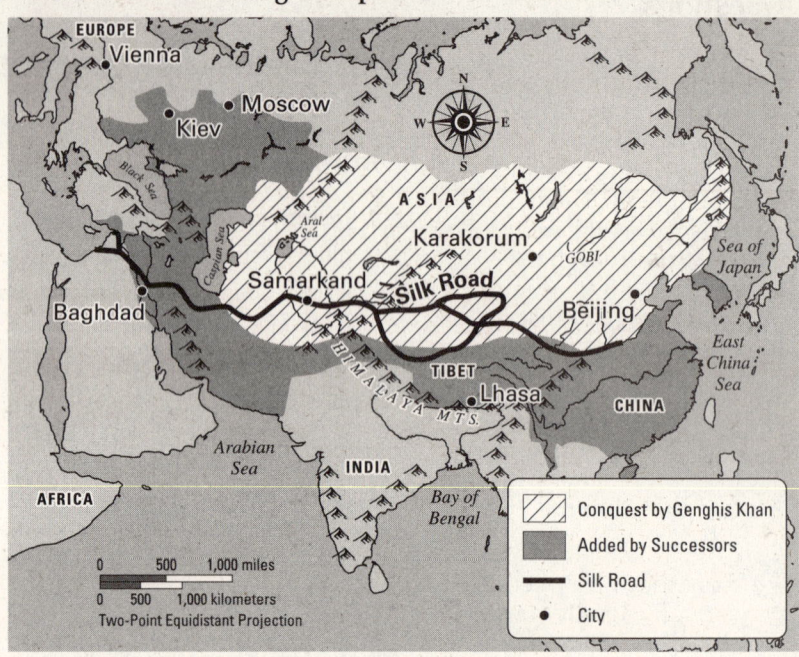

What route linked the Mongol Empire to Europe? What was the main purpose of this route?

The Silk Road; as a trade route between Asia and Europe.

Document 3: The Great Khan's Wealth

. . . All those who have gems and pearls and gold and silver must bring them to the Great Khan's mint. . . . By this means the Great Khan acquires all the gold and silver and pearls and precious stones of all his territories [lands]. . . .

. . . The Great Khan must have, as indeed he has, more treasure than anyone else in the world. . . . All the world's great [rulers] put together have not such riches as belong to the Great Khan alone.

—Marco Polo, *The Travels of Marco Polo* (c. 1300)

Why do you think Marco Polo's travels made Europeans want to see East Asia?

Europeans were interested in the treasure of the Great Khan and East Asia.

❺ **Part 2: Essay**
Write an essay discussing how the Mongols conquered Central and East Asia and how their rule affected Europeans' lives. Use information from the documents, your short answers, and your knowledge of social studies. ❻

PRACTICE

Strategies for Test Preparation

United States History Sample

Introduction

Historical Context: The first half of the 19th century was an era of tremendous physical growth for the United States. The nation expanded farther westward and seized new territory by way of negotiation, clashes with Native Americans, and wars with other countries.

Task: Analyze the key events, attitudes, and changes surrounding the westward expansion and territorial growth of the United States.

Part 1: Short Answer

Study each document carefully and use your knowledge of United States history to answer the questions that follow.

Document 1: The Louisiana Purchase and Explorations, 1804–1807

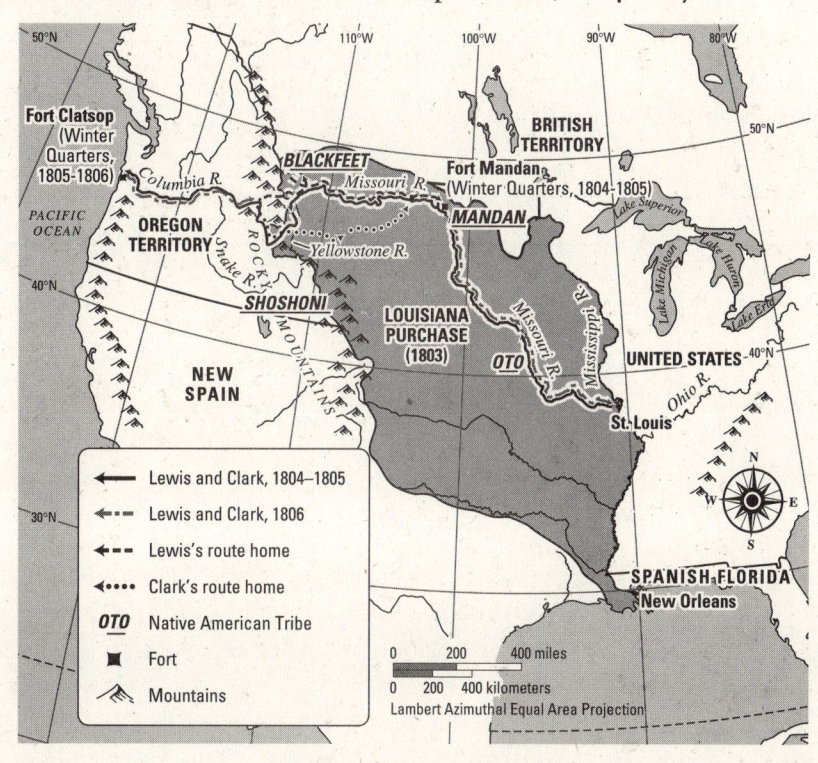

1. What effect did the Louisiana Purchase have on the physical growth of the United States?

2. What impact would acquiring the Louisiana Purchase lands have on the people already living there?

Document-Based Questions written by Dominic Fruscello, West Genesee High School, Camillus, New York

PRACTICE

Strategies for Test Preparation

Document 2: A Warning from Tecumseh

The whites are already nearly a match for us all united, and too strong for any one tribe alone to resist; so that unless we support one another with our collective and united forces; unless every tribe unanimously combines to give a check to the ambition and avarice [greed] of the whites, they will soon conquer us apart and disunited, and we will be driven away from our native country and scattered as autumnal leaves before the wind.

—Tecumseh, Shawnee Chief, 1810

1 What action does Tecumseh urge his fellow Native Americans to take?

2 Why does Tecumseh fear the whites?

PRACTICE

Strategies for Test Preparation

Document 3: Removal of Native Americans, 1820–1840

Southeastern People Relocated

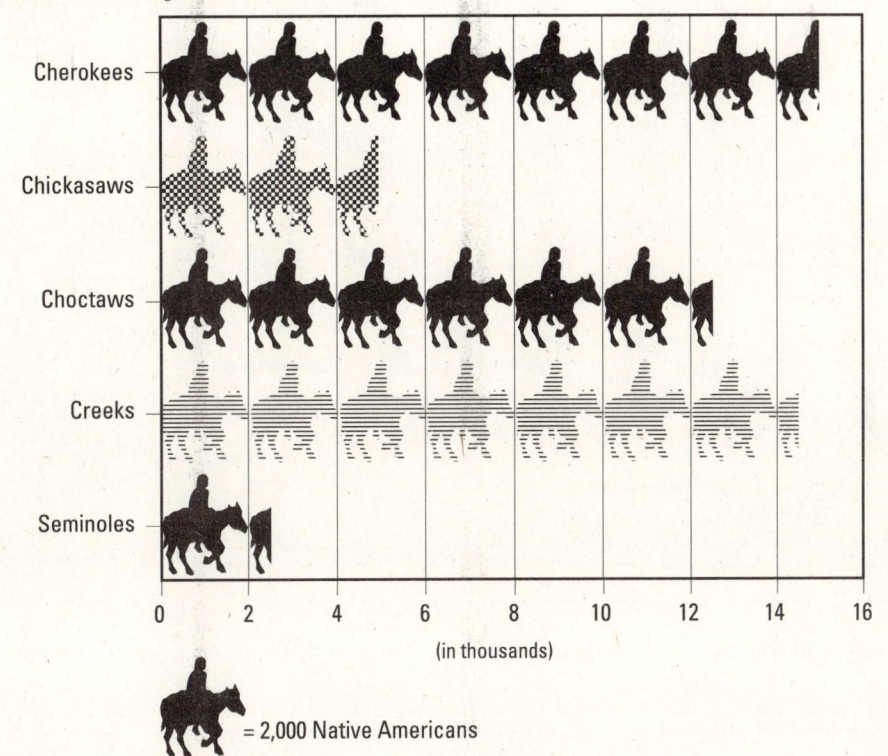

Cherokees, Chickasaws, Choctaws, Creeks, Seminoles

(in thousands)

= 2,000 Native Americans

1. Roughly how many Cherokees were relocated to western lands?

2. Approximately how many Southeastern People were relocated?

Part 2 Test-Taking Strategies and Practice **61**

Name _____ Date _____

PRACTICE

Strategies for Test Preparation

Document 4: Roads and Canals, 1812–1850

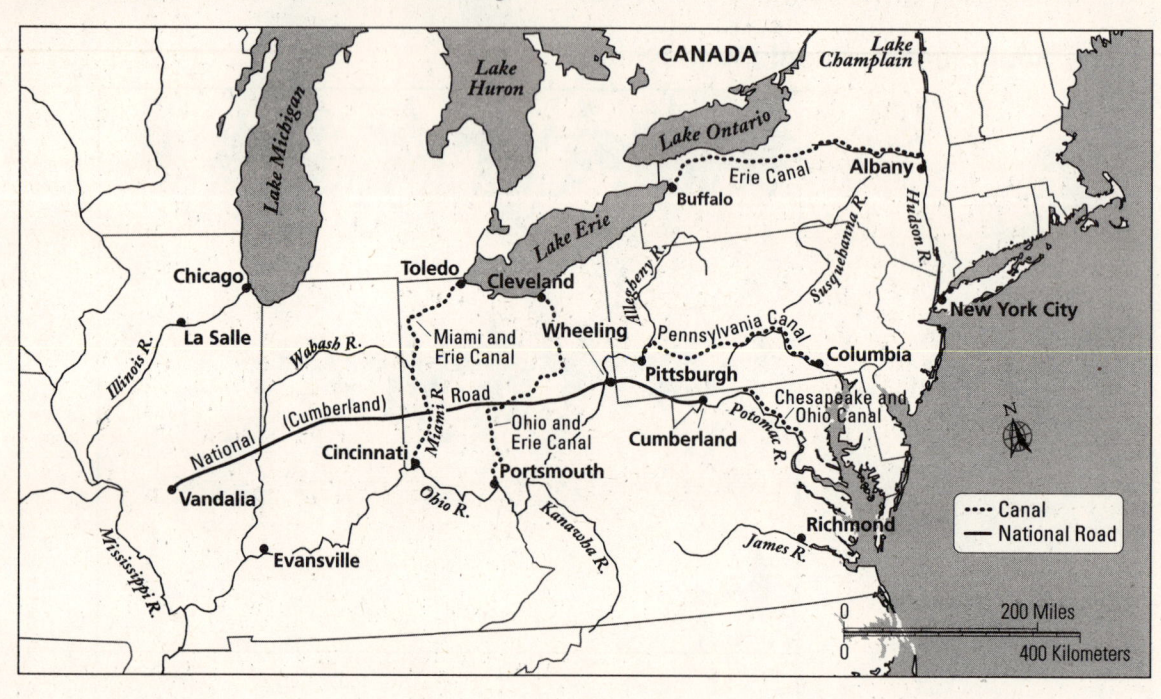

1. Based on the map, how did canals help to link the different regions of the country?

   _____
   _____
   _____

2. Why was the National Road important to transportation during this time period?

   _____
   _____
   _____

Name _____   Date _____

PRACTICE   Strategies for Test Preparation

Document 5: Trails West, 1850

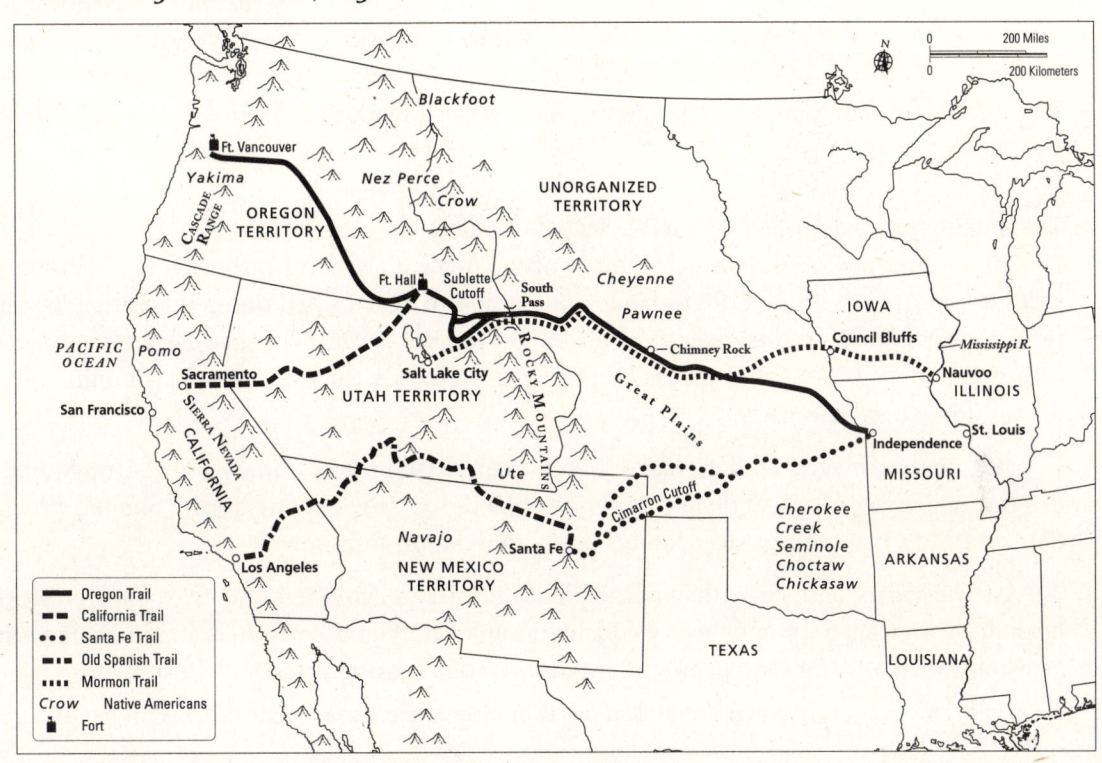

1. How did creation of major trails help in the settlement of the West?

   _____
   _____
   _____

2. What impact might the trails have had on the Native American peoples who lived in the West?

   _____
   _____
   _____

PRACTICE

Strategies for Test Preparation

Document 6: Manifest Destiny

Our manifest destiny [is] to overspread and possess the whole of the continent which Providence [God] has given us for the development of the great experiment of liberty and . . . self-government.

—John O'Sullivan, United States Magazine and Democratic Review, 1845

1. According to the notion of manifest destiny, to what land is the United States entitled? Why?

Document 7: President Polk's War Message to Congress

In my message at the commencement of the present session I informed you that upon the earnest appeal both of the Congress and convention of Texas I had ordered an efficient military force to take a position "between the Nueces and the Del Norte." This had become necessary to meet a threatened invasion of Texas by the Mexican forces, for which extensive military preparations had been made. . . .

But now, after reiterated menaces, Mexico has passed the boundary of the United States, has invaded our territory and shed American blood upon the American soil. She has proclaimed that hostilities have commenced, and that the two nations are now at war.

As war exists, and, notwithstanding all our efforts to avoid it, exists by the act of Mexico herself, we are called upon by every consideration of duty and patriotism to vindicate with decision the honor, the rights, and the interests of our country.

Source: Richard Hafstadter: *Great Issues in American History: James K. Polk, War Message to Congress*

1. According to Polk where does the blame lay for the outbreak of war? Why?

2. Why might Mexican forces want to invade Texas?

64 STRATEGIES FOR TEST PREPARATION

PRACTICE

Strategies for Test Preparation

Document 8: The Growth of San Francisco

1847   1850

Source: Victor Prevost, View of San Francisco (1847)   Source: Bancroft Library San Francisco, 1851

1 How do the dual images represent San Francisco's explosive growth in the wake of the California gold rush?

_____

_____

_____

2 How is the growth of San Francisco similar to the growth of California at this time?

_____

_____

_____

Part 2 Test-Taking Strategies and Practice **65**

Name _____ Date _____

PRACTICE
Strategies for Test Preparation

Document 9: U.S. Expansion, 1846-1853

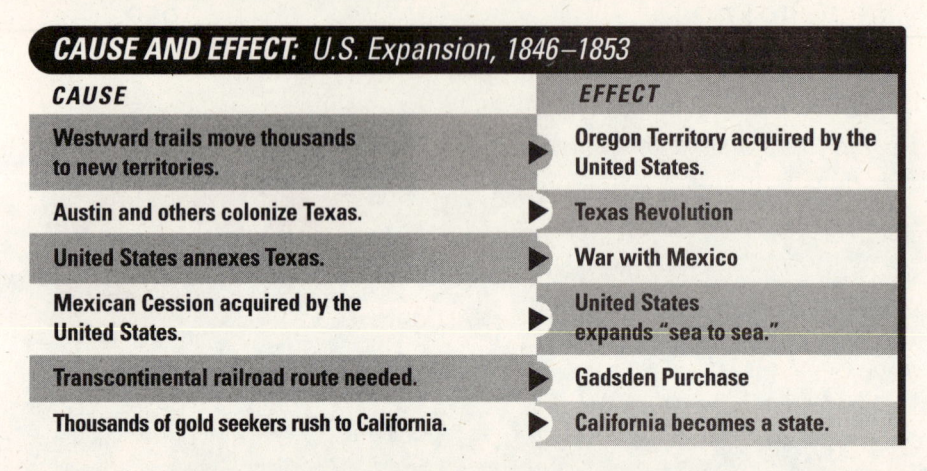

CAUSE AND EFFECT: U.S. Expansion, 1846–1853

CAUSE	EFFECT
Westward trails move thousands to new territories.	Oregon Territory acquired by the United States.
Austin and others colonize Texas.	Texas Revolution
United States annexes Texas.	War with Mexico
Mexican Cession acquired by the United States.	United States expands "sea to sea."
Transcontinental railroad route needed.	Gadsden Purchase
Thousands of gold seekers rush to California.	California becomes a state.

Source: U. S. Bureau of the Census, *Statistical Abstract of the United States: 1993*, Washington D.C. 1993, p. 180

1. How is it clear from the chart that Texas defeated Mexico in the Texas Revolution?

    _____
    _____
    _____

2. How do you think the gold rush helped California to become a state?

    _____
    _____
    _____

Part 2: Essay

Using information from the documents, your answers to the questions in part 1, and your knowledge of U.S. history, write an essay that explains the significant events and attitudes surrounding the westward expansion of the United States.

_____
_____
_____
_____
_____
_____

66 STRATEGIES FOR TEST PREPARATION

Name _____ Date _____

ANSWERS

Strategies for Test Preparation

Thinking Through the Items

Below you will find the answers to the short answer questions on the Practice pages.

Part 1: Short Answer

Document 1
1 It roughly doubled the size of the nation.
2 The land was occupied by Native Americans, who now became a part of the United States, even though they were not consulted.

Document 2
1 He wants them to unite and work as one to stop the continuing encroachment by white settlers.
2 He believes they will take the Native Americans' land.

Document 3
1 15,000;
2 about 49,000

Document 4
1 The Erie Canal helped transport goods between New York and the western part of the country, while the two canals through what is today Ohio helped facilitate trade between the North and South.
2 The National Road expanded transportation into areas not connected by canals or major rivers.

Document 5
1 They gave travelers a path to follow and made it easier for groups to navigate through the unfamiliar and often harsh terrain of the West.
2 The trails brought many settlers to the land. This probably forced the Native Americans to move away from those lands or to fight to keep the settlers out.

Document 6
1 the entire North American continent—from the Atlantic to the Pacific oceans; because God has deemed it so

Document 7
1 He lays the blame with Mexico by insisting that its forces invaded U.S. territory and killed Americans.
2 Mexico might want to regain part of Texas, which the Mexican government controlled until the Texans won their independence and then went on to become a U.S. state.

Document 8
1 They show San Francisco's transformation from a quiet and sparsely populated community to a crowded and built up city in a matter of only several years.
2 California grew rapidly as a result of the gold rush and was ready for statehood by 1850.

Document 9
1 The next entry states that the United States annexed Texas, something the nation could not have done if Texas was still under the control of another country.
2 With an influx of so many gold seekers, California reached the necessary population level to apply for statehood.

Part 2 Test-Taking Strategies and Practice **67**

Name _____   Date _____

ANSWERS   *Strategies for Test Preparation*

Thinking Through the Items

Part 2: Essay

PRE-WRITING ESSAY CHECKLIST

☐ 1 Have I read the historical context and task carefully so I understand what I am supposed to be writing about?

☐ 2 Have I read each of the documents?

☐ 3 Can I establish a relationship or links between some or all of the documents?

☐ 4 Have I thought of a topic sentence and a basic outline for my essay?

☐ 5 Do I have a conclusion for my essay?

RUBRICS

The best essays will link all the documents into a coherent examination of the changes in the United States as a result of westward expansion. First, the essay will identify the lands that were added (Document 1). It should point out that motivation for continuing westward expansion was fueled by the idea of Manifest Destiny (Document 6). The essay should mention that some lands were gained peacefully (Document 1), and some were gained through war (Document 7). The clashes between settlers and Native Americans illustrates the impact of western settlement on the Native American peoples living in the lands of the West (Documents 2,3). Next, the essay should analyze the influence of transportation on the settlement of the west (Documents 4, 5). The canals, roads, and trails facilitated the exchange of goods and people between the eastern and western parts of the United States. The essay should have a logical conclusion that summarizes the points made in the body of the composition.

POST-WRITING CHECKLIST

☐ 1 Do I have a topic sentence for my essay?

☐ 2 Do my points follow in logical succession?

☐ 3 Do I have a summary and conclusion for my essay?

☐ 4 Have I checked and corrected grammar, spelling, and punctuation errors in my work?

68 STRATEGIES FOR TEST PREPARATION

Name _____   Date _____

SAMPLE TEST

Strategies for Test Preparation

Part 3: Test Practice

Sample Test

The questions that follow illustrate the types of items found on many tests or formal assessments. Use these questions as models for preparing for tests. After you have taken the test, check the answers on pages 86–87. If you find you consistently miss one type of question return to the strategies pages in Part 2 and review the techniques for answering the type of questions you missed.

HISTORY

Strategies for Test Preparation

1. Why would John Peter Zenger have thought he could complain in his newspaper about New York's governor without being arrested?
   - A Because of rights granted by the Magna Carta
   - B Because of Parliament's policy of salutary neglect
   - C Because of rights granted by the English Bill of Rights
   - D Because New York had an elected colonial assembly

2. The high-grade tobacco that the Jamestown colonists learned to grow and sell for a profit was first developed by
   - A John Rolfe.
   - B John Winthrop.
   - C Sir Walter Raleigh.
   - D John Smith.

3. What effect did the immigration of the mid-1800s have on the United States?
   - A Cities became overcrowded, leading to unhealthy conditions and increased crime.
   - B Nativists called for laws to toughen citizenship requirements and to ban foreign-born people from running for public office.
   - C Immigrants settled sparsely populated lands and performed jobs that few other Americans would do.
   - D All of the above are true.

4. How did transportation improvements in the 1800s affect the nation?
   - A They encouraged national unity by linking distant places.
   - B They created larger markets for products.
   - C They made the movement of people and products cheaper and easier.
   - D All of the above

HISTORY

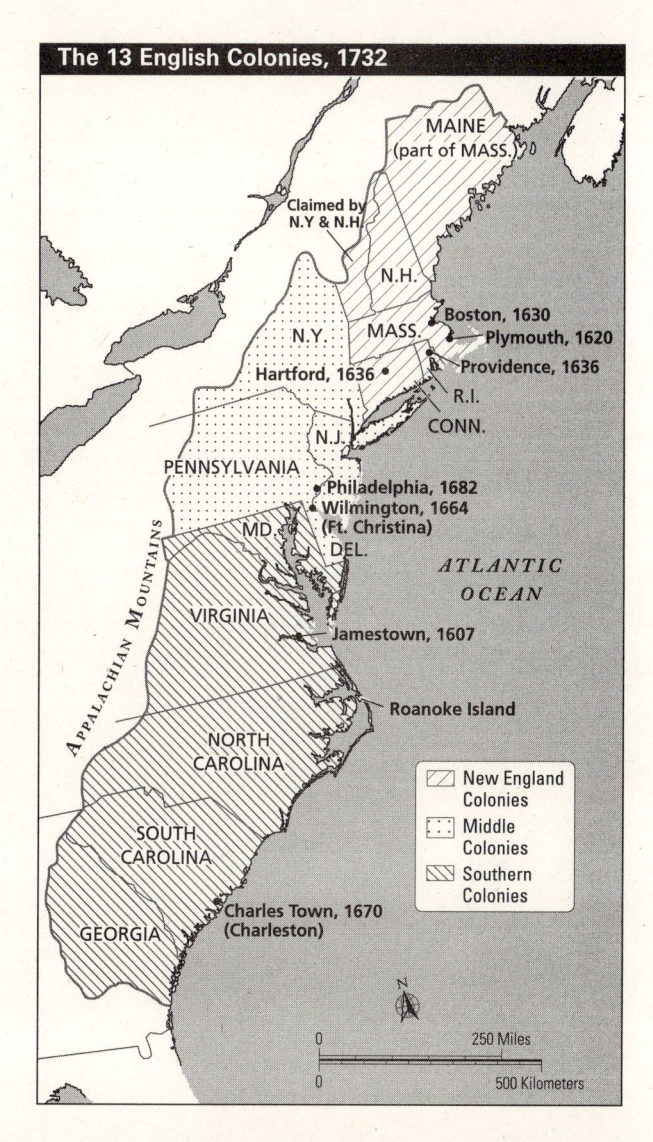

Strategies for Test Preparation

The 13 English Colonies, 1732

- MAINE (part of MASS.)
- Claimed by N.Y & N.H.
- N.H.
- Boston, 1630
- MASS.
- Plymouth, 1620
- N.Y.
- Providence, 1636
- Hartford, 1636
- R.I.
- CONN.
- N.J.
- PENNSYLVANIA
- Philadelphia, 1682
- Wilmington, 1664 (Ft. Christina)
- MD.
- DEL.
- APPALACHIAN MOUNTAINS
- VIRGINIA
- Jamestown, 1607
- ATLANTIC OCEAN
- Roanoke Island
- NORTH CAROLINA
- SOUTH CAROLINA
- Charles Town, 1670 (Charleston)
- GEORGIA

Legend:
- New England Colonies
- Middle Colonies
- Southern Colonies

0 — 250 Miles
0 — 500 Kilometers

5. Which region had the greatest number of early settlements?

    A The New England colonies

    B The middle colonies

    C The southern colonies

    D Roanoke Island

6. Select one of the three groups of colonies and describe the earliest settlements in the region.

Region: _____

The earliest settlements in the region:

_____

_____

_____

Origin of the first settlers in the region:

_____

_____

_____

_____

Part 3 Test Practice

HISTORY

Strategies for Test Preparation

7. Which of the following was a foreign-policy issue faced by Washington during his presidency?
   - **A** Immigrants to the United States criticized the government's policies.
   - **B** Farmers revolted against the government in the Whiskey Rebellion.
   - **C** The Spanish caused problems between Native Americans and settlers.
   - **D** All of the above were foreign policy issues faced by Washington.

8. Why did European nations want to colonize the Americas?
   - **A** Colonies were a good source of slave labor.
   - **B** Colonies could provide goods to enrich the home country.
   - **C** European nations were overcrowded and needed a place to send people.
   - **D** Colonies could serve as bases for ships bound for Asia.

If men were angels, no government would be necessary. . . . In framing a government which is to be administered by men over men, the great difficulty lies in this: you must first enable the government to control the governed; and in the next place oblige it to control itself.

---

9. Which of the following men most likely wrote the words above?
   - **A** Jonathan Edwards, "Sinners in the Hands of an Angry God"
   - **B** Benjamin Franklin, *Poor Richard's Almanack*
   - **C** James Madison, *The Federalist* "Number 51"
   - **D** Thomas Paine, *Common Sense*

A	Alexander Graham Bell patents the telephone
B	Robert Fulton launches a steamboat on the Hudson River
C	The Italian engineer Guglielmo Marconi patents the radio
D	Telegraph line connects Washington, D.C., and Baltimore

---

10. Which is the correct sequence for the technological developments given above, in order from earliest to most recent?
    - **A** A, B, C, D
    - **B** B, C, A, D
    - **C** B, D, A, C
    - **D** D, C, B, A

72 STRATEGIES FOR TEST PREPARATION

Name _____   Date _____

GEOGRAPHY   **Strategies for Test Preparation**

11. The purpose of gridlines on a world map is to
   - **A** separate one country from another.
   - **B** indicate longitude and latitude.
   - **C** indicate how many miles are covered in one inch.
   - **D** show roads, rivers, and canals.

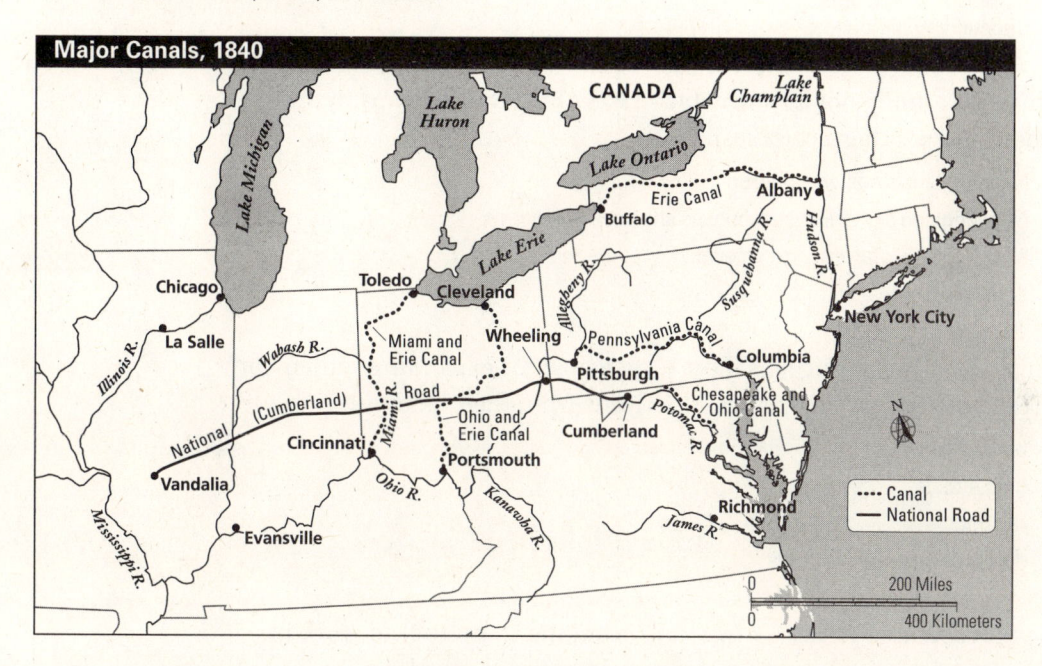

Major Canals, 1840

12. According to the map shown above, what is the most direct water route to use to take goods from Cincinnati to Albany?
   - **A** Miami River to National Road, then to Atlantic Ocean, and up the Hudson River
   - **B** Ohio River to Miami and Erie Canal, then to Lake Erie and finally to Lake Ontario
   - **C** Miami River to Ohio River, to Ohio and Erie Canal, then to Lake Erie and to Erie Canal
   - **D** Miami River to Miami and Erie Canal to Lake Erie to Erie Canal.

13. According to the map shown above, what water route would goods take going from Cincinnati to Albany?

_____
_____
_____
_____
_____
_____

Part 3 Test Practice **73**

GEOGRAPHY

Strategies for Test Preparation

14. One development that led to the rise of civilizations in the Americas was
    - A the use of animal skins for clothing.
    - B the domestication of plants and animals.
    - C the use of weapons.
    - D the building of houses.

15. Why was farming not as profitable in New England as it was in the Middle and Southern colonies?
    - A New England's soil was poorer.
    - B New England's growing season was shorter.
    - C New England's farms were smaller.
    - D All of the above are true.

16. Which of the following was most responsible for expanding settlement in the West and forcing Native Americans from their land?
    - A barbed wire
    - B gold strikes
    - C railroads
    - D disappearing buffalo herds

17. The movement of African Americans from the south to find work in the cities of the north between 1910 and 1920 was called
    - A the Trail of Tears.
    - B the Great Exodus.
    - C the Dispersion.
    - D the Great Migration.

Name _____   Date _____

GEOGRAPHY

Strategies for Test Preparation

> On July 9, on a narrow trail eight miles from Fort Duquesne, fewer than 900 French and Indian troops surprised General Braddock's forces. George Washington suggested that Braddock's men break formation and fight from behind the trees, but Braddock would not listen. The general held his position and had four horses shot out from under him. In the end, nearly 1,000 of his men were killed or wounded, and General Braddock died from his wounds. American colonists were stunned by Braddock's defeat.

18. The passage above describes a battle during which war?
    - **A** French and Indian War
    - **B** Revolutionary War
    - **C** King Philip's War
    - **D** The Civil War

19. What conclusion can you draw from the paragraph above about why Braddock was defeated in this battle?

    _____
    _____
    _____
    _____

Name _____   Date _____

GEOGRAPHY

Strategies for Test Preparation

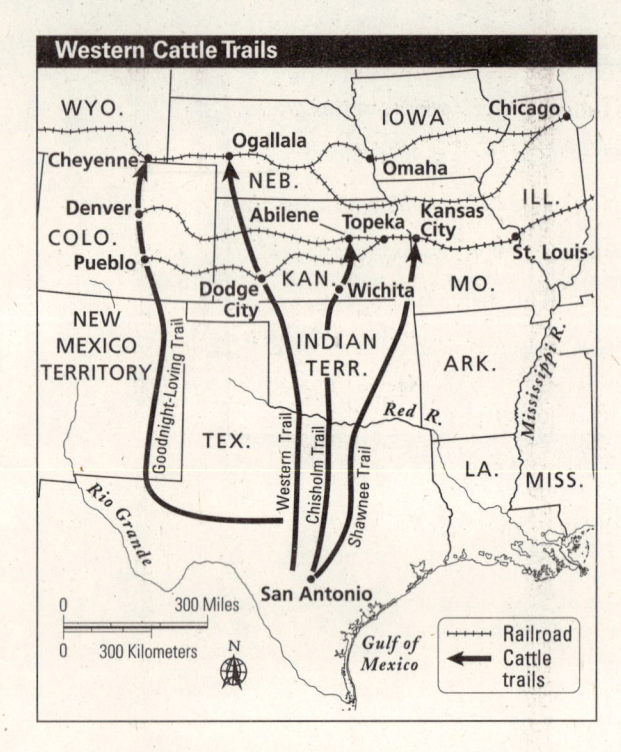

Western Cattle Trails *(map showing cattle trails from San Antonio through Texas to Dodge City, Abilene, Ogallala, and Cheyenne, with railroads and cities including Denver, Pueblo, Wichita, Topeka, Kansas City, St. Louis, Omaha, Chicago)*

20. Once they reached the Western Trail, how far would cowhands from a ranch on the Red River have to drive cattle to reach Dodge City?
    A About 1,200 miles
    B About 700 miles
    C About 300 miles
    D About 100 miles

21. What happened to the cattle at the end of the cattle trails?
    A They were shipped to cities in the east.
    B They were slaughtered and processed
    C They were sold for as much as ten times their original price
    D All of the above

22. The Land Ordinance of 1785 established a plan for dividing Western territory for sale to settlers. In what way did the plan benefit individuals who wanted to settle on the land?
    A It divided townships into parcels affordable by individuals.
    B It established a militia to protect settlers on the frontier.
    C It raised large amounts of money for the federal government.
    D It granted each settler a small parcel of land for free.

Name _____ Date _____

CIVICS AND GOVERNMENT Strategies for Test Preparation

23. Which of the following is true about the principle of judicial review, which was established in the 1803 decision in *Marbury* v. *Madison?*
    A It gave the executive branch the power to review the Supreme Court's decisions.
    B It made the Supreme Court more important than the other two branches of government.
    C It gave the Supreme Court the right to amend the Constitution.
    D It gave the Supreme Court the power to declare laws unconstitutional.

24. Which of the following is not a right guaranteed to citizens under the Constitution?
    A The right of an employed person to keep his or her job
    B The right of an accused person to refuse to testify against himself or herself
    C The right of a person to practice his or her own religion
    D The right of a newspaper to publish unpopular opinions

25. The power "to lay and collect taxes, duties, imposts and excises, to pay the debts and provide for the common defense and general welfare of the United States" belongs to
    A Congress.
    B the president.
    C the Supreme Court.
    D the military.

26. Which of the following groups could not vote in colonial government elections?
    A Native Americans
    B Women
    C Enslaved persons
    D All of the above

27. The main relationship between a trial court and an appellate court is that
    A a case is first heard in an appellate court, and the results may be appealed to a trial court.
    B a case is first heard in a trial court, and the results may be appealed to an appellate court.
    C a complicated case bypasses a trial court and goes directly to an appellate court.
    D civil cases are heard in a trial court and criminal cases in an appellate court.

Part 3 Test Practice **77**

CIVICS AND GOVERNMENT
Strategies for Test Preparation

> Fifteenth Amendment
>   (1870; concerning African Americans)
>
> Nineteenth Amendment
>   (1920; concerning women)
>
> Twenty-sixth Amendment
>   (1971; concerning 18-year-olds)

28. The three Constitutional amendments named above all concern
    - A taxation.
    - B voting rights.
    - C national defense.
    - D prohibition.

29. Which of the following methods was used by civil rights advocates to achieve their goals?
    - A boycotts
    - B lawsuits and court cases
    - C sit-ins and demonstrations
    - D all of the above

30. The idea of spreading political power to all the people and ensuring majority rule in the early 1800s was called
    - A Popular Sovereignty.
    - B Manifest Destiny.
    - C Jacksonian Democracy.
    - D Era of Good Feelings.

CIVICS AND GOVERNMENT

Strategies for Test Preparation

Ratification of the Constitution		
State	Convention Vote	Month/Year Ratified
Delaware	30–0	December 1787
Pennsylvania	46–23	December 1787
New Jersey	38–0	December 1787
Georgia	26–0	January 1788
Connecticut	128–40	January 1788
Massachusetts	187–168	February 1778
Maryland	63–11	April 1788
South Carolina	149–73	May 1788
New Hampshire	57–47	June 1788
Virginia	89–79	June 1788
New York	30–27	July 1788
North Carolina	194–77	November 1789
Rhode Island	34–32	May 1790

Source: *Encyclopedia of American History*

31. What information on the chart above might explain why Rhode Island was the last state to ratify the Constitution?

  A The Rhode Island convention had fewer delegates than any other state's convention.
  B Rhode Island ratified the Constitution by a larger margin than any other state.
  C The vote in the Rhode Island convention was unanimous.
  D The vote at the Rhode Island convention was closer than in any other state.

32. What reason might be given for the convention votes being closer as the date reaches 1790?

  A People began to have more information about the Constitution.
  B More people voted at the conventions.
  C There was greater opposition to the Constitution in the South.
  D None of the above.

Part 3 Test Practice

ECONOMICS

Strategies for Test Preparation

33. In an economic system, interest is paid by
    - A loan customers to a bank over and above the amount of the loan.
    - B banks to customers on the balance in savings accounts.
    - C customers to credit card companies on the unpaid balance of their accounts.
    - D All of the above.

34. Congress passed the Social Security Act in 1935 in order to
    - A provide employers with a new means of screening prospective employees.
    - B give jobs to people who had been out of work for more than six months.
    - C provide workers with unemployment insurance and retirement benefits.
    - D accomplish All of the above.

35. Industry in the Midwest saw explosive growth during the 1800s mainly because of
    - A transportation and natural resources.
    - B a large, skilled, unemployed work force.
    - C rich soil and inexpensive vacant land.
    - D the mild, dry climate of the region.

36. How did improvements in the sewing machine affect the clothing industry?
    - A Job opportunities for women increased.
    - B Mass-produced clothing became available in standard sizes and styles.
    - C The industry declined and workers lost jobs.
    - D More people began to make their own clothes at home.

37. In what ways did people in the 1920s differ from Americans before them?
    - A They became more interested in leisure activities and having fun.
    - B Some questioned the values of the past and traditional ways of doing things.
    - C They spent more money on items and activities that were not necessities.
    - D All of the above.

ECONOMICS

Strategies for Test Preparation

Home Ownership

Median Family Income
(adjusted for inflation)

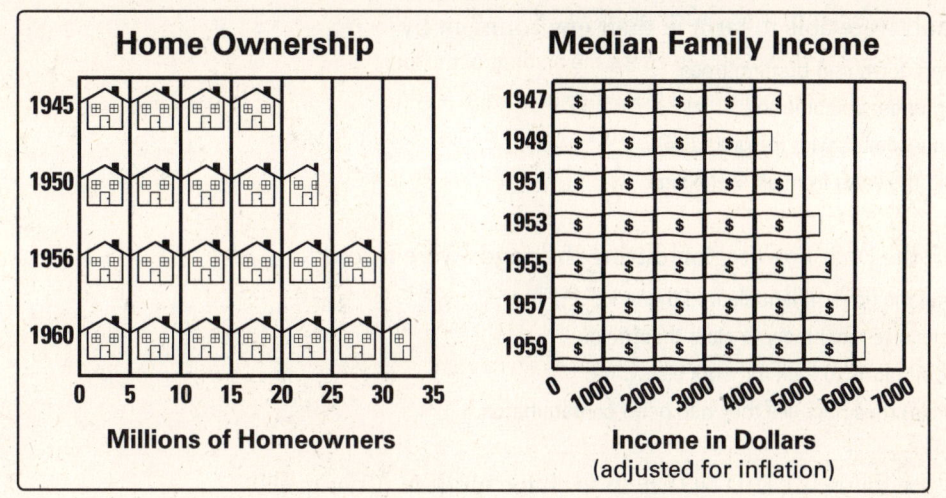

Source: *Historical Statistics of the United States*

38. What relationship between median family income and home ownership is shown in the graphs?

    A Family income rose as fast as home ownership.
    B Home ownership was not affected by increases in median family income.
    C As family income rose, so did home ownership.
    D Homes cost more in 1960 that they did in 1945.

39. What reason might be given for low home ownership in 1945?

    A The Depression wasn't over.
    B World War II was still going on.
    C Banks were loaning money.
    D People preferred renting a home to owning a home.

CULTURE

Strategies for Test Preparation

40. The Iroquois were able to farm in their environment by
    A chopping down and burning trees.
    B plowing under volcanic soil.
    C filling in wetlands with rocks and soil.
    D scraping the sand from alluvial plains.

41. Farmers in the Dust Bowl region during the 1930s were forced to
    A wait until the government cleared the land.
    B buy expensive machinery to clear their fields.
    C leave their farms to look for work elsewhere.
    D burn their crops because they had been contaminated.

42. Which of the following DID NOT help to shape modern American mass culture?
    A sports
    B political machines
    C music
    D advertising

43. In the 1950s, when the baby boom created a need for more housing, where did many Americans find new housing?
    A the suburbs of large cities
    B small rural towns
    C the west coast of the country
    D crowded slums in the inner cities

Name _____ Date _____

CULTURE

Strategies for Test Preparation

Ancestry of Americans, 1990	Descendants (in millions)
1. German	58
2. Irish	39
3. English	33
4. African	24
5. Italian	15
6. Mexican	12
7. French	10
8. Native American	9
9. Polish	9
10. Dutch	6

Refer to the chart above to answer the following questions.

44. The majority of immigrants came from which continent?
- A Asia
- B Africa
- C Europe
- D South America

45. Which of the groups would you expect to increase most rapidly in the near future because of new immigration?
- A Native American
- B German
- C African
- D Mexican

Part 3 Test Practice **83**

CULTURE

Strategies for Test Preparation

> The first time the colonies met to consider acting together in protest, the delegates drew up a petition to the king protesting the Stamp Act. The petition declared that the right to tax the colonies belonged to the colonial assemblies, not to Parliament. Later, colonial merchants organized a boycott of British goods. The boycott meant they refused to buy the goods.

46. Based on the passage above, why do you think the colonists believed the Stamp Act was wrong?

   A The boycott was hurting their businesses.
   B The king had the right to tax the colonies but Parliament did not.
   C Colonial assemblies, not the king, had the right to tax colonies.
   D The Stamp Act did not raise enough money for the colonies.

47. Based on the passage above, why do you think the colonists decided to boycott British goods?

   A They wanted to promote American made goods.
   B They hoped the loss of the trade from the boycott would force the British to repeal the act.
   C They hated the king and wanted to force him out of office.
   D It was the only way they had to protest.

CULTURE

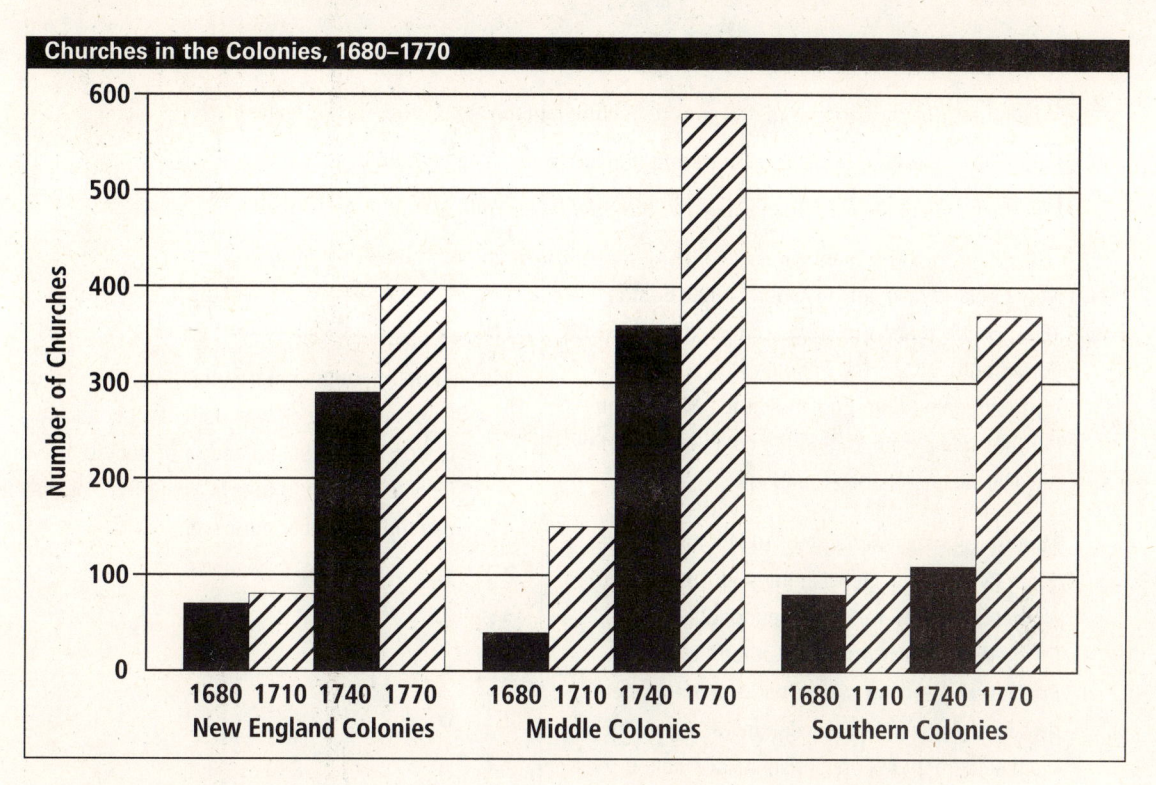

Strategies for Test Preparation

Churches in the Colonies, 1680–1770

[Bar graph showing Number of Churches (0–600) for New England Colonies, Middle Colonies, and Southern Colonies at years 1680, 1710, 1740, and 1770]

48. Which region shown in the graph saw the greatest increase in churches between 1680 and 1770?

   A The New England colonies
   B The Middle colonies
   C The Southern colonies
   D It is impossible to tell from the graph

49. Which region shown in the graph saw the greatest increase in churches between 1740 and 1770, at the time of the Great Awakening?

   A The Southern colonies
   B The Middle colonies
   C The New England colonies
   D Similar growth occurred in all three regions.

ANSWER KEY

Strategies for Test Preparation

1. C
2. A
3. D
4. D
5. A
6. New England colonies: Plymouth, 1620; Boston, 1630; Hartford and Providence, 1636. (Not shown, Portsmouth, 1623). The Pilgrims who settled at Plymouth came from England on the Mayflower; Puritans came from England to colonies started by the Massachusetts Bay Company.

    Middle colonies: Wilmington, 1664; Philadelphia, 1682. (Not shown, New Netherland, 1624.) New Netherland (New York) was founded by the Dutch West India Company; Dutch, Jewish, English, and African people came among others. Swedes founded New Sweden in 1654, with its main settlement at Fort Christina, later called Wilmington. English Quakers led by William Penn founded Pennsylvania.

    Southern colonies: Roanoke Island, 1585, 1587; Jamestown, 1607; Charles Town(Charleston), 1670. (Not shown, Maryland, 1632; Carolina, 1663.) English settlers led by Sir Walter Raleigh tried to settle at Roanoke Island. The Virginia Company of London financed the colony at Jamestown, bringing English settlers. Lord Baltimore established Maryland for Roman Catholics fleeing persecution in England. Charles Town was built by English settlers from Barbados.
7. C
8. B
9. C
10. C
11. B
12. D
13. The National Road moved goods into areas not connected by canals.
14. B
15. D
16. C
17. D
18. A
19. Although he had more men than the enemy force, General Braddock was defeated because his troops were exposed and unprotected; he was not flexible enough to take Washington's advice and use the vegetation for cover.
20. C
21. D
22. A
23. D
24. A
25. A
26. D
27. B
28. B
29. D
30. C
31. D
32. A
33. D
34. C
35. A
36. B
37. D
38. C
39. B
40. A

Name _____ Date _____

ANSWER KEY

Strategies for Test Preparation

41. **C**
42. **B**
43. **A**
44. **C**
45. **D**
46. **C**
47. **B**
48. **B**
49. **A**